PRAISE FOR *THE SUBURBAN CHRISTIAN*

"What an education. Al Hsu's excellent book inspires me to see the place in which I live with new clarity, creativity and gratitude. He expanded my imagination and enlarged my heart for the city near us, and God's world around us. I hope every suburban Christian will read it."

KELLY MONROE KULLBERG, FOUNDER OF THE VERITAS FORUM AND AUTHOR OF *FINDING GOD BEYOND HARVARD*

"With no end in sight for suburban sprawl and urban challenges spreading relentlessly outward from the city core, *The Suburban Christian* is right on time. Don't run from the suburbs, Al Hsu urges—redeem them. It's a message whose time has come."

ROBERT D. LUPTON, AUTHOR OF *THEIRS IS THE KINGDOM* AND *RENEWING THE CITY*

"*The Suburban Christian* is a helpful, needed resource for living thoughtfully and faithfully in suburbia. Al Hsu has researched well, thought hard and lived vulnerably to produce what I believe will become a basic primer for all believers who live in suburbia. There are no easy answers here, though. By thoughtfully deconstructing suburbia (I'll never look at malls or roads or sidewalks exactly the same way again) and by honestly wrestling with what it is like to live in suburbia (finely highlighting the tensions, ironies and surprises of life here) Al Hsu gives me a clearer, deeper understanding of the life I live and helps me ask the right questions about how to live as a suburban believer."

DON EVERTS, AUTHOR OF *JESUS WITH DIRTY FEET* AND *GOD IN THE FLESH*

"Albert Hsu has written a readable and well-researched treatment of a key issue. I live and work in the exurb, and I am grateful for his wisdom."

JOHN ORTBERG, AUTHOR OF *IF YOU WANT TO WALK ON WATER, YOU'VE GOT TO GET OUT OF THE BOAT*

"A very important book for all of those who are seeking to faithfully follow Jesus in the suburbs. A candid grappling with both the challenges and the opportunities of suburban living. A great resource for church study groups."

TOM SINE, AUTHOR OF *THE MUSTARD SEED CONSPIRACY* AND *LIVING ON PURPOSE*

"Provocative, thoughtful, even prophetic, *The Suburban Christian* is a book the church badly needs."

LAUREN F. WINNER, AUTHOR OF *GIRL MEETS GOD* AND *REAL SEX*

"This book is a long-overdue pilgrimage through the empty promises, hidden hopes and subtle demons of suburbia. Urban cynics and suburban hermits rejoice—here is a refreshing invitation to find God at work in the margins, the same God who showed up in the unlikely badlands of Nazareth from which the world said nothing good could come."

SHANE CLAIBORNE, AUTHOR OF *THE IRRESISTIBLE REVOLUTION*

THE
SUBURBAN
CHRISTIAN

**FINDING SPIRITUAL VITALITY
IN THE LAND OF PLENTY**

Albert Y. Hsu

IVP Books

An imprint of InterVarsity Press
Downers Grove, Illinois

For more about suburban Christianity, see Al Hsu's blog:
www.thesuburbanchristian.blogspot.com

InterVarsity Press
P.O. Box 1400, Downers Grove, IL 60515-1426
World Wide Web: www.ivpress.com
E-mail: mail@ivpress.com

InterVarsity Press® is the book-publishing division of InterVarsity Christian Fellowship/USA®, a student movement active on campus at hundreds of universities, colleges and schools of nursing in the United States of America, and a member movement of the International Fellowship of Evangelical Students. For information about local and regional activities, write Public Relations Dept., InterVarsity Christian Fellowship/USA, 6400 Schroeder Rd., P.O. Box 7895, Madison, WI 53707-7895, or visit the IVCF website at <www.intervarsity.org>.

Scripture quotations, unless otherwise noted, are from the New Revised Standard Version of the Bible, *copyright 1989 by the Division of Christian Education of the National Council of Churches of Christ in the USA. Used by permission. All rights reserved.*

The "Blessing" from "Morning Prayer" in Celtic Daily Prayer *from the Northumbria Community is used by permission.*

Design: Cindy Kiple
Images: Paxton/Getty Images

ISBN-10: 0-8308-3334-X
ISBN-13: 978-0-8308-3334-4

Printed in the United States of America ∞

Library of Congress Cataloging-in-Publication Data

Hsu, Albert Y., 1972-
The suburban Christian: finding spiritual vitality in the land of
plenty / by Albert Y. Hsu.
*   p. cm.*
Includes bibliographical references.
ISBN-13: 978-0-8308-3334-4 (pbk.: alk. paper)
ISBN-10: 0-8308-3334-X (pbk.: alk. paper)
1. Christianity and geography—United States. 2.
Suburbanites—United States—Religious life. 3. Sacred space. 4.
Materialism—Religious aspects—Christianity. 5. Consumption
(Economics)—Religious aspects—Christianity. 6. Human geography.
I. Title.
BR115.G45H78 2006
223.09173'3—dc22

                                                              2006004130

| **P** | 19 | 18 | 17 | 16 | 15 | 14 | 13 | 12 | 11 | 10 | 9 | 8 | 7 | 6 | 5 | 4 | 3 | 2 | 1 |
| **Y** | 20 | 19 | 18 | 17 | 16 | 15 | 14 | 13 | 12 | 11 | 10 | 09 | 08 | 07 | 06 | | | | | |

For Ellen,

best friend, beloved wife,
and former small-town girl
who never thought she'd be
living in the suburbs.

Thanks for joining me on this
suburban adventure.

CONTENTS

INTRODUCTION

Suburbia—Paradise or Wasteland?

The suburban life is a spiritual quest.

I had been researching the topic of suburbia for well over a year before this idea crystallized in my mind. In recent years, new suburbs have emerged as edge cities, the new metropolises that stand independently outside older cities in places that just a decade ago were often empty farmland or desert. These suburbs are the latest version of the promise of the American frontier—blank slates on which new residents can write their stories. The pioneers who move to these suburbs "have made a startling leap into the unknown," writes commentator David Brooks. "The places have no past, no precedent, no settled conventions. The residents have no families or connections here."[1] But people move here with the hope that there soon will be communities and relationships developed among people in the same boat as themselves. Fellow pilgrims on the journey, as it were.

I was struck by the significance of suburban living as a spiritual quest or pilgrimage. We're all here looking for something. People live in suburbia for any number of reasons. We may have come here because of a job change or for a relationship. We come in search of affordable housing, good schools or safe communities. Or we may have grown up in suburbia by default; indeed, over half of the American population now lives in suburbia, and many of us have been suburbanites for two or three generations. Whatever the case, we who live in suburbia have aspirations for a certain kind of life. For some it is an optimistic vision, while others may be more cynical about ever seeing such a life come to be. But it is still a spiritual longing in either case.

Even those who come to suburbia for less than noble reasons do so out of a particular vision of their ideal life. Some move to suburbia out of fear of those unlike them, fleeing from racial diversity and searching for a place "safer" and more comfortable to their preexisting prejudices. Others care little for their neighbors and fashion suburban lives of self-centered materialism, acquisition of possessions and status climbing. These too point to spiritual needs, however misguided or impure the motivations might be.

Whenever people describe suburbia, invariably they use phrases like "a good place to raise kids" or "where people settle down and start a family." Inherent in these comments is an aspiration of hope for their future and a dream of a good life for their children. In other words, suburbia is the context and the setting for the fulfillment of people's hopes and dreams.

The very geography of suburbia, especially new development, provides people with the opportunity for a fresh start, a second chance. For the recent college graduate, the new divorcee, the refugee and immigrant, the suddenly widowed or downsized or retired, a move to or within suburbia represents the search for another life. It is a contemporary version of the huddled masses yearning to breathe free. It is as if today's transient, mobile population is taking heed of the words of the apostle Paul: forgetting what is behind, straining toward what is ahead. The old is gone, the new is come. Suburbia can be seen as a place for redemption from the past and of hope for the future.

What is the suburban dream? What do the suburbs offer? Respite from wandering in the wilderness and the possibility of a promised land, perhaps. Historians Rosalyn Baxandall and Elizabeth Ewen observe:

The suburbs had always promised prosperity, upward mobility, a healthy life in an unpolluted environment, safety and tranquility, and above all, the best place to bring up kids. Although this promise still fuels many dreams and infuses a nostalgic political rhetoric, the future is in doubt. Although most Americans today live in the suburbs, the elements of the covenant are elusive. What remains for many is a sense of quiet despair and faint hope.[2]

A mix of despair and hope is as good as any description of the suburban ethos. We are here in suburbia because we have some notion that it's a good place to be, but we are beginning to question exactly how good it is for us. We find ourselves experiencing a kind of suburban ambivalence.

It seems that much of what we long for in life, whether community and family, security and shelter, love and happiness, or meaning and purpose, is embodied somewhere in the suburban landscape. Looking for friends? There are people here by the millions. Searching for a place to call home? Subdivisions as far as the eye can see. Need work to do? Plenty of jobs in suburbia. Want material stuff? Anything you can imagine is at a mall or big-box store near you. It's all here.

Yet many of us still haven't found what we're looking for. Instead of an idyllic paradise or restful haven, suburban living is often hectic and frazzled. Instead of a place of community, suburbia is often anonymous and isolated. We find ourselves frustrated with our commutes, lacking time with friends and family, trapped by debt and consumerism. The suburban world, far from an Edenic garden or American dream, often seems to be more of a fallen world. *Utopia* literally means "no place," and it may seem like the suburban utopia is nowhere to be found. Living in such a material environment, we begin to suspect that suburbia may be detrimental to our spiritual lives. We feel spiritually impoverished in the midst of this land of plenty. Can we truly experience God in the suburbs? Is it possible to live authentic Christian lives as suburban Christians?

THE LEGITIMACY OF SUBURBAN LIVING

Suburban residents sometimes find themselves caught between both urban and rural ideals. On the one hand, suburbia can be seen as inferior to the urbane, cosmopolitan, cultured world of life in the big city. On the other hand, compared to the pristine wilderness and natural beauty of rural settings, suburbia can seem artificial, plastic and shallow. Either way, suburbia comes up short.

Christianity Today once ran a cover story called "Suburban Spirituality." The article raised some thought-provoking observations about the spiritual challenges of suburban life. More jarring, however, were the letters to the editor that ran a few issues later. For example, one person wrote:

> The Christian life is about divestiture, not acquisition. It is the laying aside of every weight in order to run the race. You can do this in the city or the wilderness, but in the affluent suburbs, it can be done only in the most enfeebled and rudimentary way. The final irony is that many young Christians move to the suburbs and take on suffocating commutes and mortgages for the benefit of their children. This amounts to placing children at the very epicenter of the world's value system—materialism—and then expecting to grow a Christian child.[3]

Another letter writer likewise wrote, "The fact is that the suburbs are Prozac for the soul. Can you really be intimate with the living God when your senses are dulled, your time is not your own, and the cost to stay in the game keeps mounting? I'm not so sure."[4]

Is this true? Was my spiritual health endangered merely by living in the suburbs? Suburbia certainly affects its dwellers in myriad unnoticed ways, but these letter writers were essentially saying that suburbia is antithetical to the Christian life. They implied that suburban Christians are more shallow, vapid or materialistic than other Christians. If they were correct, then I cannot fully live out the Christian life as an authentic follower of Jesus, just because I happen to live in suburbia.

While raising some good points, these letter writers were critiquing a particular kind of suburban life without being open to the possibility that true Christians could indeed live faithfully in suburbia. I felt somewhat defensive and took their comments personally because I have always lived in suburbia. I was born in one of New York City's boroughs and grew up in a suburb of Minneapolis. I now live in the western suburbs of Chicago. It's the air I breathe, and like many other suburbanites I have something of a love-hate relationship with the suburbs. For better and for worse, I am a suburbanite. It's who I am, how I see life, how I experience the world.

Behind the readers' comments is a tacit assumption that the Christian life simply can't be lived in certain environments. While it is certainly true that different settings will lead to differences in how the Christian life is lived, we should not assume that faithful Christian living in the suburbs is by definition impossible. Rather, the challenge for suburban Christians is to discern how they might avoid the pitfalls of suburban life and be authentic Christians in this very setting. Just as Christians have struggled to be faithful to God wherever they have been—in Jerusalem or Rome, in medieval or colonial times, in agrarian or industrial societies, in urban centers or on the wild frontier—so too must Christians develop a thoroughly Christian approach to living in contemporary suburbia. The suburban Christian ought not uncritically absorb all the characteristics of the suburban world but rather should thoughtfully assess and discern how Christians ought to live in this environment, without either capitulating to the culture or abandoning it by fleeing the suburbs and relocating to the country.

Indeed the problems and challenges of suburban living are significant, as the following chapters will explore. But for Christians, nothing is beyond redemption. Over the past few years I have increasingly realized that suburbia has affected me in ways I am only beginning to understand. There's no escaping that suburbia has profoundly shaped who I am, and more specifically, *suburbia has shaped my Christian experience.* I understand my faith differently than I would have if I had grown up in rural or urban settings. As we examine how suburbia has influenced our Christian practice for good and for ill, we will consider ways that Christians can redeem the suburbs. How has suburbia shaped our Christianity, and how might Christianity shape the suburbs?

Given that so many Christians dwell in the suburbs, we can take hope in the possibility that suburbs can become key centers of vibrant Christian faith and life. Suburbs are neither to be avoided nor to be preferred. Just as Christians are present in both rural and urban settings, I will simply take as a given that Christians are likewise present in suburbia and *should* be present in suburbia. Thus we need to develop a Christian perspective to suburban living.

I should say at the outset that my scope is necessarily selective. Suburbia is a huge, complex topic, and multiple books have been written on each of the various issues in this book. So I don't claim to be exhaustive or to have the authoritative word on suburbia. I'm not a professional sociologist or cultural analyst, just a fellow suburbanite wanting to make sense of our world. My task has been to read and distill some of the existing literature and research on suburbia so you don't have to tackle it all yourself.

So let's examine suburbia with some of the tools that sociologists, historians, cultural anthropologists and missiologists use to understand a culture. What makes suburbs tick? Why are they the way they are? What are suburban people like? What does it mean to be a suburban Christian? And how might Christian faith contextualize itself in such a way as to be compelling to suburbanites without getting sucked into the trappings and temptations of suburban living?

If you are interested in these kinds of questions, welcome. Consider this a Christian guided tour of suburbia. We'll look beyond the stereotypes of suburbia as either shallow wasteland or utopian paradise and instead reckon with both the opportunities and challenges facing suburban Christians. May this suburban safari be helpful to you in your spiritual pilgrimage.

The Suburban Moment

Glimpses of a Suburban Future

By 1970, more Americans lived in suburbs than in either central
cities or rural areas. By 2000, more Americans lived in suburbs than
in central cities and rural areas combined. The United States had
become a predominantly suburban nation.

DOLORES HAYDEN, *BUILDING SUBURBIA*

Suburbia is significant. Why? Because more people live in suburbia than ever before, and if trends continue, society will increasingly become more and more suburban. In 1950 less than a quarter of America's population lived in suburbia. By 2000, over half did. Urban cores have plateaued or are declining, while the suburbs continue to expand and grow at amazing rates.[1]

While demographers and missiologists often speak of the world's urban future, it may be equally accurate in many postindustrial societies to talk about the suburban future. With the majority of the population living in suburbs, much of the focus of future mission work and ministry outreach will necessarily be in suburban areas. Indeed, in a relatively short period of a half century or so, suburbia has emerged as the dominant cultural context of North America.[2]

Suburbs are no longer "sub." Today, "not only are Americans more likely to live in a suburb than in a city, town, or farm; they are also more likely to work in a suburb, shop in a suburb, and attend entertainment and sports events in a suburb."[3] This has displaced the former centrality of the cities. David Brooks writes, "We have a huge mass of people who not only don't live in the cities, they don't commute to the cities, go to movies in the cities, eat in the cities, or have any significant contact with urban life. They are neither rural, nor urban, nor residents of a bedroom community. They are charting a new way of living."[4]

"Today more Americans live, work,
go to schools and colleges, and do their shopping
and recreation in suburbs than in cities."

J. JOHN PALEN, *THE SUBURBS*

Given suburbia's new centrality, Christians, especially suburban Christians, must take the suburbs seriously. If Christians are to herald the presence of the kingdom of God in our suburban contexts, we need to think about what suburbia is and how it works. Only when we understand how it affects us can we think about how we can affect suburbia.

A SUBURBAN JOURNEY

I grew up in the suburbia of the 1970s and 80s. My hometown, Bloomington, was Minneapolis's largest suburb, with a population of about 82,000. Public parks were abundant there, with plenty of woods, lakes, bike trails and beaches. In the frigid Minnesota winters, my friends and I went sledding, skiing and ice skating, built snow forts and had snowball fights. In the summers we played cops and robbers around our cul-de-sac and built tree forts in the nearby woods. Some of my fondest memories are of warm afternoons playing sandpit volleyball with high school friends.

My suburban hometown was a place of in-betweenness. If I drove twenty minutes one way into the city, I'd be in downtown Minneapolis, able to visit skyscrapers or museums, see live theater or catch a Twins baseball game at the Metrodome. If I drove twenty minutes in the opposite direction, I'd be in the country, with dairy farms and barns dotting the landscape. In between these two worlds was my world—suburbia.

Bloomington can be roughly divided between east and west. The two high schools drew their students from their respective sides of the city. East Bloomington was an older community, representing earlier suburbs that were developed in gridlike formation akin to traditional city centers and small towns. West Bloomington, on the other hand, was newer development, with winding roads and larger lots. At the far edge of the city limits was "*prestigious* west Bloomington," with million-dollar homes on hills overlooking the lakes. My high school classmates came from a variety of income brackets, ranging from blue-collar to executive status. My own suburb, while mostly middle- to middle-upper class, was a microcosm of several different socioeconomic classes and housing models in close geographic proximity.

I went to college in Rochester, Minnesota, home of the Mayo Clinic. Rochester is a city of about 85,000 people, located about an hour and a half south of the Twin Cities. It stands on its own as a city big enough to have many of the amenities of city life, yet it's close enough to the Twin Cities should you have a hankering for anything you couldn't find in Rochester. Minnesotans are famously proud of being nice and providing nice communities to live in. For several years Rochester ranked number one in *Money* magazine's top places to live in the United States, and Minneapolis-St. Paul ranked in the top five. Rochester has been described as "a suburb looking for a city." Perhaps that's why I felt so comfortable there during my college years. It reminded me of the suburb I'd grown up in.

Many of my college classmates and friends, on the other hand, found Rochester too big and even threatening. Most had come from small towns across Minnesota and neighboring Midwestern states. I was one of the few students from a metropolitan area, and my high school of two thousand was bigger than some of their hometowns. So I was called a "city kid" by my rural counterparts. I would correct them and say, "I'm not from the city. I'm from the suburbs." This was an important distinction in my mind, even though it all seemed the same to them.

My suburban identity was such that I didn't want to be thought of as being from the city. I had a few classmates from inner-city Minneapolis, and their experience growing up seemed far removed from my own. I also wanted to distance myself from the small-town mindset of my rural friends. Back then I had a rather condescending attitude toward both urban and rural environments. I saw myself as a cultured, cosmopolitan-minded suburbanite. I was proud of the fact that my high school had ranked second in the state in terms of overall academic, artistic and athletic programming. I was sure that my educational experience was superior to what my classmates had received in their smaller rural schools or underresourced urban schools. I assumed that my suburban identity made me more accomplished and ambitious than my peers.

I didn't realize then how wealth and privilege factored into different school districts' ability to provide resources for their students. I probably perpetuated my classmates' conceptions of suburbanites being snobby and superficial. It wasn't until meeting friends from different geographic and socioeconomic backgrounds that I realized that I had a certain sense of entitlement and superiority that tainted how I viewed others. And yet I was grateful for the benefits and advantages I had received from growing up in the suburbs. Had suburbia been good or bad for me? Did it make me a better person or a worse one? Or both?

Even then I began to wonder: *If I'm neither a "country bumpkin" nor a "city slicker," then what am I? What are suburbanites? Is there such a thing as a suburban worldview? What does it mean to be suburban?*

I also remember several classes at my Christian college that focused on the need for urban ministry on both a domestic and global level. Classic urban ministry textbooks like Ray Bakke's *The Urban Christian* emphasized the strategic significance of cities for Christian mission and ministry. Our college encouraged students to have ministry internships in inner-city settings, both here and overseas. But in practice, most of the school's involvement was among its supporting churches in rural Minnesota. Though the majority of the population lived in urban and suburban centers, I wasn't seeing a proportionate emphasis on ministry and church planting in metropolitan areas.

After college, I moved to Illinois for graduate school and have lived in the western suburbs of Chicago ever since. In Minnesota, suburbia seemed neatly defined, distinctly located between city and country. In northern Illinois, however, suburbia seems to be the dominant form of landscape. In some parts of Chicagoland, you can drive for an hour in any direction and still be in the suburbs. Because of distance and traffic, it takes me an hour to get downtown, so I rarely visit the city. It is now quite infrequent for me to experience either urban life in the big city or rural life in the small town. For me and my family and millions of others, suburbia is inescapable. We live in a suburban world.

DEFINING SUBURBIA

Defining suburbia is both a simple as well as a tremendously complicated task, and sociologists have employed different kinds of definitions, typologies and classifications. At a most basic and functional level, suburbia is that seemingly self-evident area that is neither urban nor rural and usually is situated between central cities and unincorporated open land. If you're not living in the city limits proper of an urban metropolis like New York, Toronto or Seattle but are living in a community either adjacent to a city or several contiguous municipalities away, then you probably live in suburbia.

There are also multiple kinds of suburbs and tremendous diversity between suburbs. Some are older communities with a historic small-town feel, while others are new developments with little sense of history. Some are primarily blue-collar and industrial, while others are mostly white-collar and professional. Some are historically African American or other ethnicities, while many are still mainly white. Different regions of the country also have their own personalities and characteristics. So we must beware of making sweeping overgeneralizations about suburbia.

On the other hand, surprisingly, suburbs share similarities even across all these differences. Historian Kenneth T. Jackson, in his landmark study *Crabgrass Frontier*, found that suburbs across the country have common traits of population density, homeownership, residential status and journey-to-work that give them strong commonalities in ethos and lifestyle, regardless of geographic region.[5] In many ways a suburb of Houston has more in common with a suburb of Atlanta or Denver than it does with an urban or rural community in the same state.

The prefix *sub* in *suburb* has often been understood to indicate a community's dependence on the larger urban center near it. It was not urban, but *suburban*. *Urban* was understood as having the central institutions of commerce, industry, government and arts. Suburban areas lacked some or all of these elements, and suburban residents would routinely travel to

---

"The sprawling suburbs now account for more office space than the inner cities in every metro area in the country except Chicago and New York."

DAVID BROOKS, ON PARADISE DRIVE

---

the urban center to work, shop or participate in cultural events.

This no longer holds as a rule of thumb. While a good percentage of corporations and jobs are still found in downtown central business districts, suburban job growth has meant that workers from cities and inner-ring suburbs now commute outward rather than inward. And we may bypass our own cities entirely. Some years I make more trips to Los Angeles, Orlando or Nashville than I do to downtown Chicago, and often the closest I get to the city is O'Hare or Midway airports.

In some metropolitan areas, the newest suburbs are called exurbs. The prefix *ex* in *exurban* indicates both "out of" the city as well as "formerly of" the city. They are no longer "sub," in that these new exurban edge cities are often economically autonomous and no longer dependent on the older cities. Those in exurbia are looking for all the resources of the city without having to be in the city. People don't quite know what to call these new suburban-urban hybrids; they have been called technoburbs, superburbia, exurbs or perimeter cities. Just a few decades ago they were cornfields or empty desert; now they are bustling centers of commerce and power.[6]

California's Silicon Valley is an example of the new exurbia. It is "suburban in form—sprawling, patternless—but it is a city in function. It is a center of wealth, business, industry, finance, education, and research."[7] The Valley is a cluster of technoburbs that are more important to the regional economy than either of the adjacent older cities of San Francisco or San Jose. A one-thousand-square-foot bungalow in Palo Alto can run $600,000. Ironically, San Francisco is becoming a bedroom community to Silicon Valley, as Valley residents find themselves priced out of affordable housing.[8]

People continue to search for certain ideals: a good place to live with maximum positive opportunities and minimum negative liabilities. As a result, suburbs and exurbs are becoming the dominant new form of city.[9] But the new suburbanism is far more complex than that.

THE SUBURBANIZATION OF CITIES

Cities have had suburbs growing around them from the start. But increasingly, cities themselves are taking on suburban traits, especially in layout and organization. One historian writes, "After almost two centuries of steady growth, suburbs have overwhelmed the centers of cities, creating metropolitan regions largely formed of suburban parts. . . . In the spaces of the suburban city lie metropolitan complexities."[10] The familiar concept of an urban core with suburban rings around it is becoming less and less the norm. While this previous model is familiar in older East Coast cities such as Boston or Washington, D.C., it is less common in newer cities in the south and west.

By the turn of the twenty-first century, most population centers had moved to the new reality of "multicentered metropolises." Outer cities are not extensions of the old "core-periphery" model of cities and suburbs; today's suburban centers are a new organizational model entirely.[11]

"Parts of the city are actually becoming suburbs to the suburbs."

ALEX MARSHALL, *HOW CITIES WORK*

For example, Los Angeles can be thought of as a suburban metropolis. The geography of southern California has not lent itself to Los Angeles proper as being "central" in any meaningful way. In fact, the region's commerce and industry is decentralized and spread out across multiple smaller cities and suburbs.[12]

Joel Garreau, author of *Edge City,* observes, "Every single American city that is growing, is growing in the fashion of Los Angeles, with multiple urban cores."[13] As the decentralized cityscape continues to unfold, more cities will be developed with suburbanlike land-use patterns in mind—sprawling rather than concentrated in a dense central district, more dependent on the automobile rather than public transit or pedestrian walkways. Cities, especially the newest ones, are themselves changing to look more and more like suburbs.

THE URBANIZATION OF SUBURBIA

At the same time, suburbia is urbanizing in two directions. On the one hand, the newest suburbs, exurbs and edge cities are taking on the civic traits of cosmopolitan centers by providing the kinds of features once only found in urban centers. But on the other hand, many of the oldest suburbs are increasingly becoming like the cities they are adjacent to. While poverty is still disproportionately concentrated in central cities, in recent years urban renewal and gentrification has been dislocating the poor. As low-income urban neighborhoods are redeveloped for middle-income and upscale professionals, public and low-income housing is being eliminated, forcing the poor to move toward less affluent communities at the edges of cities. In other words, as community developer Robert Lupton puts it, "poverty is suburbanizing."[14]

According to a 1999 U.S. Department of Housing and Urban Development report, older inner-ring suburbs are experiencing many of the same problems as urban cities, such as job loss, population decline, crime and disinvestment. These older suburbs have a declining tax base, aging population, increasing poverty and deteriorating schools and infrastructure.[15]

Even as new suburbs become new cities, old suburbs become old cities. Urban blight is becoming suburban blight. Increasingly, suburban issues are urban issues, and we will need all the experience and strategies of urban renewal and community development to attend to the changes in the urbanizing suburbs.

THE SUBURBANIZATION OF RURAL AREAS

Another recent trend in suburbanization is that suburbs are not only growing out from the cities, but they are also growing in from the outside. Small towns now have suburbs too.

The U.S. Census Bureau formerly categorized small cities as "non-metropolitan" areas. Now a new term, "Micropolitan Statistical Areas," designates areas with a central city between 10,000 and 50,000 people. Such cities and their suburbs may carry a combined population and commercial power of 150,000 to 200,000 people. These small towns are growing in clout. For example, Roanoke Rapids, North Carolina, is a small city of 17,000 and less than eight square miles. But the micropolitan area that it anchors has more than 76,000 people and 1,360 square miles. Such micropolises are increasingly targeted by national department store and restaurant chains as potential places for growth. "Branding these places recognizes what Wal-Mart has known for years: It doesn't take a big city to create an urban economy."[16]

As a result, rural areas now have suburbs. The suburban developments growing around small cities look much like the suburbs of big cities. They have similar development and land-use patterns as well as nationally branded retail and commercial outlets. A resident of a micropolitan suburb will likely feel quite at home in a metropolitan suburb and vice versa. While there are still stark cultural differences between the landscape of a small town and a big city, the rural suburb and the urban suburb are much the same. The primary difference is in real-estate values, but this is only a difference in degree, not in kind.

In terms of land-use patterns, rural suburbs can be even more suburban than urban suburbs. The vast amount of open land around small micropolitan cities means that their suburbs can be situated miles away, creating a spread-out commuter culture. Robert Lang, director of the Metropolitan Institute at Virginia Tech, says, "Micros are more suburban because they're born sprawling." Lang's research shows that more than half of the land area in the continental United States lies in either metropolitan or micropolitan areas. "Rural areas now for the first time make up the minority share."[17]

DeKalb, Illinois, is a micropolitan city of about 40,000 and home to Northern Illinois University. It's about a half-hour drive west of the far western edges of the Chicago suburbs. At the edge of DeKalb's adjacent "suburb" of Sycamore (population 12,000), there are plenty of new developments, with subdivisions of recently built townhouses and new shopping areas complete with national chains. Borders, Barnes & Noble, Pier 1

Imports, Ruby Tuesday, PetSmart. While many local mom-and-pop establishments still exist, clearly the national corporations have targeted the DeKalb micropolitan area as an area of growth. They see this and other micropolitan cities like it as home to future shoppers and customers.

Small-town life, for better or for worse, is disappearing. As rural suburbs come to resemble metropolitan suburbs, micropolitan areas are repositioning themselves as smaller communities that offer the benefits and opportunities of suburban life without the problems of bigger cities. The growth of micropolitan suburbs is yet another indicator of the dominance of suburban culture. Whether urban or rural, suburbs are inescapable.

THE SUBURBAN SHIFT

Suburbs have existed in some sense throughout human history. Four thousand years ago, the Sumerian community of Ur in southern Mesopotamia had a population of 100,000 that spilled beyond the city's gates. John Wycliffe used the word *suburbis* in 1380, and Chaucer used it in *The Canterbury Tales* a few years later.[18] In North America, Boston, Philadelphia and New York had suburbs well before the Revolutionary War.

Yet suburbs are also a fairly modern development. In America, the mid- to late-nineteenth century saw a huge demographic shift from the country to the city, and suburbs as we now think of them began to emerge. A second major shift, from city to suburbs, occurred in the mid-twentieth century. Modern mass suburbia came to the fore after World War II. Ever since, the percentage of people living in the cities has declined and the percentage of suburbanites has increased.[19]

In previous eras, cities were the civilized centers of society, and suburbs tended to be dangerous slum areas. A diary entry from 1849 records, "Nine-tenths of those whose rascalities have made Philadelphia so unjustly notorious live in the dens and shanties of the suburbs."[20] Both in the United States and in Europe, suburbs housed the societal outcasts. Shakespeare's Globe Theater was located outside of London proper, across the Thames in the suburbs, reflecting the marginalization of theaters and actors. In Elizabethan England, brothels moved to outer areas, so prostitutes were known as "suburban sinners." It was an insult to call someone "a suburbanite." The *Oxford English Dictionary* in the nineteenth century defined a suburb as "a place of inferior, debased, and especially licentious habits of life."[21]

A primary way that North American cities and suburbs differ from their counterparts around the world is in the distribution of socioeconomic classes. In most cities around the world, the wealthy live in the city centers, while the poor live in the "suburbs." From Cape Town to Cairo, Barcelona to Rome, Bombay to Paris, the metropolis is where quality housing and public services are provided, usually at an economic premium. In many international cities suburban areas are usually lower-income, with slums and shantytowns found mostly around the rims.

"In 1990 the United States became the first nation to have more suburbanites than city and rural dwellers combined."

ROSALYN BAXANDALL AND ELIZABETH EWEN, *PICTURE WINDOWS*

This is the opposite pattern of American urbanization and suburbanization. In the United States, while commerce still takes place in center cities, personal wealth is more concentrated in the suburbs than in the cities. "In the United States, status and income correlate with the suburbs, the area that provides the bedrooms for an overwhelming proportion of those with college educations, of those engaged in professional pursuits, and of those in the upper-income brackets."[22] In other words, in America, even if people work in the cities, they tend to live in the suburbs, and they bring their wealth and income home with them. As Robert Lupton puts it, U.S. cities are like "donuts with a hole in the middle and the dough all around the outside."[23]

American cities and suburbs differ from their global counterparts because of the compelling historical narrative of the American frontier. In medieval Europe, the impulse was to centralize inward in the cities, since city populations needed to stay within the boundaries of defensible walls for safety from external threats. In contrast, it is a distinctly American impulse to turn one's horizons outward. Go west, young man! Westward ho! The pioneer spirit and the concept of manifest destiny motivated thousands of Americans to move away from the original thirteen colonies to stake out their own land in this new world. Even those who did not journey to Oregon or California may well have gone to Chicago or St. Louis, and even there they were likely to expand out beyond the urban cores of the center cities into the new settlements that would become the suburbs.[24]

Urban historian Joel Garreau notes that America has experienced three major waves of suburbanization. The first wave was *residential*. After World War II the postwar baby boom of the 1940s and 50s required the building of millions of homes outside of center cities. This introduced the concept of the bedroom community, where people live and sleep a certain geographic distance from where they work.

The second wave was *commercial*. In the 1960s and 70s, people tired of shopping downtown because it was now a lengthy drive from the residential suburbs. So stores moved out of the city, building malls and marketplaces where people lived, in suburbia. Now commerce was done in local markets, not in urban centers.

The third wave, in effect since the 1980s and 90s, has been *industrial*—the move of jobs and companies out of the city and into the suburbs. Business and commerce moved from central cores to the emerging edges. Now we work where we already live and shop.

In sum, suburbia has become the context and center of millions of people's lives, and decisions and innovations made in suburbia influence the rest of society. If Christians want to change the world, they may well do so by having a transformative Christian impact on suburbia and the people therein.

CALLED TO SUBURBIA?

As demographic patterns have morphed and people have gravitated to suburban contexts, Christians have asked serious questions about Christians and suburban migration. Are urban ills due to Christians fleeing the cities for the suburbs?

It's true that Christians bear some complicity for urban blight. Despite a rich history of Christian presence and ministry in cities, American evangelicals have tended to have a theologically insufficient view of the city. Many have seen cities as dens of evil and corruption, as if the sins of Sodom and Gomorrah were inherent to their simply being cities. Christians are just as guilty as the general population of fear, apathy and disinterest in their civic communities. It has always been a temptation to avoid challenging environments and head for the hills.

So Christian urban ministry leaders have rightly argued against this anticity impulse and have called Christians to reestablish their presence in the city. As many have pointed out, the trajectory of Scripture moves from garden to city, from Eden to New Jerusalem. This is the course of both biblical history and human civilization. The Old and New Testaments are filled with examples of God's concern for the city and its strategic missional importance.[25] Rather than seeing the city as a place to be avoided, the city is a place to be embraced, where Christians can relocate and have a ministry of presence, acting as salt, light and leaven, finding solidarity with the poor and marginalized, bringing revitalization to local communities.

Unfortunately, a side effect of this renewed emphasis on the city has been the idea that living in the city is somehow preferable or morally superior to living in suburbia. Cities are pitted against suburbs. While it may not be stated so explicitly, the implication might be that truly committed Christians live in the city, and shallow, selfish Christians live in the suburbs.

This too is an insufficient view of the city. It's just as incorrect to elevate the city to a preferred status as it is to denigrate it as evil or corrupt. Rather than contrasting cities against suburbs, it is more helpful to see cities and suburbs as part of a metropolitan whole. Our contemporary understanding of "the city" needs to include both city and suburb, and God needs Christians to have a presence throughout the entire metropolis. While an individual suburb might not be a microcosm of the total city, it is an essential slice of the larger metropolis that cannot be partitioned off or seen in isolation, just as a traditional local urban neighborhood is an essential component of the whole city. Concern for the city means concern for the suburbs and vice versa.

Ultimately both are legitimate places of Christian discipleship. Each will have different daily challenges and issues, but both are avenues and opportunities for Christian service and witness. All of us, whether rural, urban or suburban, must ask ourselves: Where do I sense God's call on my life? Where is God calling me to locate myself, and what community is he calling me to invest myself in?

I came to the Chicago suburbs for graduate school and found employment nearby. My wife and I didn't think much about the merits of living here; our jobs were in suburbia, so we lived in suburbia. But over the years we have become more rooted and invested in our local community, and we have a greater sense of God's call to this particular suburb. What was at first an arbitrary decision now presents itself as an opportunity to live out God's call in our suburban context.

Some of our colleagues who work in our suburban office have sensed a call to live in more urban environments, and part of the reality of living out that call is the tradeoff of a longer commute. Other coworkers telecommute from other areas of the country, having life situations and callings that propel them to live elsewhere. Wherever we live, we are called to live there Christianly, in ways that make sense for that setting.

Some might argue that the very idea of settling down at all, whether in suburbia or elsewhere, is unbiblical. We might look to the Old Testament stories of Israelite nomads, wanderers and exiles who were always on the move, or the New Testament example of Jesus not having a place to lay his head, or Paul's constant missionary journeys. There is certainly something to be said about being free to go wherever God might lead. Settling in suburbia may run counter to that missionary impulse.

At the same time, we can also see biblical examples of faithful people who located themselves in particular communities in order to be salt and light there. A significant Old Testament theme is the land, and family clans were to be rooted so they could have history and permanence. Even the exiles in Babylon were exhorted to settle down and build houses, to invest themselves in their local communities and to seek the welfare of their city (Jeremiah 29:5-7). The missionary impulse for many of us might well be to settle in suburbia in order to have a significant Christian presence, lest we lose our witness there.

It's one thing to live in suburbia by default without ever wondering whether God would call us to live elsewhere. Informed suburban Christians will not be ignorant of the needs of the city and may well consider relocating to a more urban environment. This is similar to the larger question of global crosscultural missions. All Christians ought to consider how God might be calling them to participate in his worldwide mission. If we aren't called to go, we must be sure that we are called to stay—not in a passive sense, but to stay with an intentionality of active sending, sharing of resources and participating in global mission even at home.

So too it is with Christians in suburbia. All of us would do well to consider whether God might use us strategically in a different context. But if we conclude that we are called to stay in suburbia, then we ought to do so intentionally, seeking out ways of participating in God's work and mission in our immediate environment, loving our neighbors and caring for the poor, whether materially or spiritually impoverished. The old slogan "Think globally, act locally" is still true. Our mindset should embrace a global perspective of mission and justice, even while we seek out God's call for us in suburbia.

Even as we consider how God might use us to serve in urban or rural areas or the uttermost ends of the earth, let's not forget the suburbs. Jonah was rebuked by God's concern for the 120,000-plus people living in Nineveh (Jonah 4:11). Shouldn't we be concerned about suburbia and the thousands and millions there? Let it not be said of our generation that we didn't seek the welfare of the suburbs!

Living in Suburbia

The Pursuit of the Promised Land

The only trouble with living in these new housing developments is there are no trees to hit your head against.

Charlie Brown, in *Peanuts*, July 28, 1956

Our former youth pastor's family moved to a new housing development in an outlying suburb. It was about half an hour west of their previous home, which is how far they needed to travel to find something in their price range. When we first visited their new house, we stood on their lawn and looked out across a wide, empty field. It happened to be a bright, sunny day, and we breathed deeply of the fresh air. The sense of open space was tremendously invigorating, in contrast to their previous living environment of tightly developed condominiums in close quarters. Here we could see more of the horizon. Each single-family house had a good-sized yard where children could run free and play. There was little traffic or ambient noise, and it was a setting of domestic safety and tranquility. I could see why people would want to move out here, despite the distance; it was a glimpse of the frontier that is only seen on the edges.

However, less than a year later more houses had been constructed in the empty fields. What had been so appealing about that new neighborhood had ironically undone itself. Now it felt more like other established suburbs. The trees were still smaller, but the feel of the community had become drastically less open than before. The roads leading to the development were busier, and the air no longer seemed as fresh. As real-estate values continue to increase, suburbia continues to expand, driving more people to move farther and farther out, in search of the ideal community.

This reminds me of an image that C. S. Lewis uses in *The Great Divorce*. There Lewis imagines a "grey town" that stretches in every direction. He could see no fields, rivers or mountains, only endless empty streets that filled the field of his vision for thousands of miles. The reason all the streets are empty is that nobody can stand each other. To avoid their neighbors, everybody keeps moving farther away. "Finally he'll move right out to the edge of the town and build a new house," leaving more and more empty streets behind.[1] What Lewis is describing is hell.

Certain aspects of suburban life could indeed seem like "suburban hell." But the opposite is also true; suburbia was created in hopes of providing a certain kind of paradise on earth. In this chapter we'll explore the building of suburbia and how housing and land development have shaped the suburban ethos.

THE PROMISE OF SUBURBIA

What drove the growth of suburbia? While suburbs can be traced back across the centuries, by the mid-twentieth century suburbia had become something more than a mere geographic or demographic entity. Suburbia became the embodiment of a dream, a vision, a promise, appealing to the longings and yearnings of its newfound residents.

A convergence of historical forces created mid-twentieth-century suburbia. During the Great Depression, highways were constructed to provide jobs and public works projects and to facilitate the growth of the automobile industry. But much urban housing deteriorated during the Depression, lacking resources to maintain infrastructure. Then, during

World War II, building materials were redirected to the war effort, perpetuating urban decay.[2] After the war, America needed millions of new housing units to accommodate all the soldiers and sailors coming home from the war. The Federal Housing Administration made large-scale home building feasible for developers, and the Servicemen's Readjustment Act of 1944 helped veterans purchase homes by preapproving them for FHA mortgages. The postwar baby boom meant that unprecedented numbers of young families needed places to live, and the Interstate Highway Act of 1956 further accelerated suburbanization and urban decentralization by providing easy transportation access in, out of and around the cities. Nine million people moved to the suburbs in the decade following the war. In 1950 the national suburban growth rate was ten times that of central cities.[3]

The predominant image of postwar suburbia is "Levittown." In 1946 Levitt and Sons transformed four thousand acres of Long Island potato fields into Levittown, a development of 17,400 one-and-a-half-story houses of 750 square feet each. Each house was built on a concrete slab and contained two bedrooms, a bathroom, a living room and kitchen, with no basement or hallways and an unfinished attic. These homes were mass production applied to housing, inexpensive, standardized and prefabricated. As one of the Levitts said, "We are not builders. We are manufacturers."[4]

The earliest Levittown suburbs were derided as being homogenous cookie-cutter patterns that stamped out individuality. But their fundamental purpose was largely noble: "The original idea of Levittown was to give home owners a piece of the American dream: an affordable house in a new suburban setting."[5] For millions of young families, Levittown and other similar developments were the fulfillment of the American dream of homeownership. Despite the architectural homogeneity, they were affordable and practical. Suburbia became the new way of life. As one analyst puts it:

They were happy to be there. This was not the city, this was an asylum from the city, and they could commute back to the city to earn their living. No more crowded city living. No more crime and grime. Here in post-World War II suburbia they had their own houses, lawns, and garages. Here, they could raise their kids in a safe, clean environment. Here, they could escape from the aftermath of the Depression, the war, and the crowded city. Suburbia answered the social need for community and homeownership felt by many Americans who desired peaceful surroundings in contrast to urban unpleasantness.[6]

Suburbia developed at a pivotal time in American history. In contrast to the hard times of the Great Depression, the postwar suburban era was one of tremendous productivity and affordable goods, modest by today's standards but nearly unbelievable luxury to the grateful inhabitants of the new suburbs. In contrast to the trauma and chaos of World War II, postwar suburbia was a peaceful place of solace and refuge. After being delivered from poverty and death, many suburbanites would have seen their new setting as a modern-day promised land.

Suburban developers deliberately used religious imagery to market their houses. Even as early as 1891, an ad for a house in a Chicago subdivision depicted an angel delivering a home for just $10 a month, saying, "The working man's reward. Where all was darkness, now is light."[7] Suburbia was often compared to Eden, and owning your own home and yard was depicted as heaven on earth. One writer comments,

> The timeless dream that unites Americans of all races, incomes and beliefs is simply having a place of their own—*home*. This is the traditional strength of the American suburbs. Anyone can have their own plot of land, and everyone is reasonably free from being told how to live their lives.[8]

This ideology of suburbia, this dream of suburbia as refuge from pain and hardship, continues to be a default setting and often an unconscious one. Even as more cynical views of suburbia come to the fore, the paradisiacal vision endures, even if only to be critiqued as shallow or mocked as empty. For the first time, perhaps, an entire generation began to consider that their ideal experience of life was not found in the urban centers, nor on the rural prairie. The suburban landscape was all anybody needed. It was a dream realized. Why ask for anything else?

OH, GIVE ME A HOME

So as we tour suburbia, we see that it naturally begins with one of the most basic of human needs—shelter. Suburban developers, architects, urban planners and builders worked to provide a growing population with a safe, secure place to live and raise their families. Fundamental to people's opportunities to live, work and fulfill their dreams is having a place to call home.

Social historians Rosalyn Baxandall and Elizabeth Ewen argue that the history of suburbia is at the heart of twentieth-century American history, and that fundamental to it is the accessibility of affordable housing.

> The idea of suburbia was central to visionaries, planners, and socially conscious architects who began to imagine a new America. In their vision suburbia meant a place where ordinary people, not just the elite, would have access to affordable, attractive modern housing in communities with parks, gardens, recreation, stores, and cooperative town meeting places.[9]

What was true of the early Levittowns is also true of today's newest exurbs and edge cities. As Garreau puts it, "These new urban areas are marked not by the penthouses of the old urban rich or the tenements of the old urban poor. Instead, their landmark structure is the celebrated single-family detached dwelling, the suburban home with grass all around that made America the best-housed civilization the world has ever known."[10]

We can affirm that in many ways, the development of suburbia has been a tremendously positive force, raising the standard of living of many and anchoring countless families with stable places to forge their lives. Suburban development has provided the context for much contemporary prosperity and economic growth.

"At first they had advertised Park Forest as housing.
Now they began advertising happiness."

WILLIAM WHYTE, ON PROMOTERS OF AN ILLINOIS SUBURB IN THE 1950s

---

Of course, the story is not without complications. Numerous problems have arisen because of suburbia, with multiple unintended consequences that public policy decisions and land planning have had on our personal and communal lives. But this is the opening act in a drama of creation, fall and redemption. We will see the fallenness of suburbia, and we will explore possibilities for redeeming suburbia. But before we critique suburbia's flaws, let's remember its creational good—that its original purpose and intent was to provide a place called home for many who were weary and heavy laden.

SUBURBAN APPEAL

Suburban life has had widespread, nearly universal appeal. Despite urban detractors who reject suburbia as inferior to city life, history shows that people from all economic classes have participated in suburban expansion. Indeed, it is hardly the case that only the middle class live in suburbia. While cities may have more visible class differences from the very poor and the very rich living in the same urban Zip Code, suburbs themselves have diversity from subdivision to subdivision.

Suburban residents are often quite satisfied with their experience. "National surveys going back several decades indicate that suburban residents have a higher degree of satisfaction with their communities than do city residents."[11] They are more likely to be satisfied with their cultural opportunities, community services, parks and schools than city dwellers.[12]

Suburbia's success is perhaps due to the idea that suburbia represents a middle ground between the urban and the rural. Historian Robert Fishman says, "Suburbia kept alive the ideal of a balance between man and nature in a society that seemed dedicated to destroying it."[13] The suburban ideal is the notion that we can have the benefits of the city without urban problems, and the peace and charm of small towns without rural isolation and backwardness. Some claim that this is the best of both worlds while others say that it is the worst of both worlds. The reality is likely more ambiguous. Suburbia, like any environment, is a mixed bag of the good and the bad.

Whatever similarities and differences it may have with urban and rural settings, suburbia is its own entity, and by its very nature it will be attractive to certain kinds of people and repulsive to others. J. John Palen reports that studies show that "suburbanites clearly and consistently indicate a preference for suburban living."[14] Suburbia is both a self-selecting and a self-perpetuating environment. Those who like suburban living are drawn to it, and many of those who are born and raised in suburbia continue to live there out of default or familiarity.

SUBURBAN HOUSING AND AMERICAN INDIVIDUALISM

Suburbia's growth has been driven by supply as well as demand. It is in many parties' economic interest to facilitate the ongoing development of suburbia. The financial solvency of a staggering number of industries depends on continued growth, including real-estate developers and agents, mortgage bankers, construction companies, contractors, architects, surveyors, designers, and engineers, not to mention retailers like The Home Depot and Ikea that supply materials and furnishings for all those homes. The multibillion-dollar home-building industry is a juggernaut that dominates political and civic concerns.

The particular *kind* of homes that are built hints at what ultimately drives the market. It's not just any housing that is most appealing to suburbanites but *single-family housing* in particular. "With no national land use policy in the United States, single-family housing has often driven suburban planning by default. Between 1994 and 2002, real estate developers completed about 1.5 million new units of housing every year, most of them suburban single-family houses."[15]

Central to suburban housing and living is the core philosophical idea of American individualism. In this notion of the American dream, the ideal is that every individual family has their own plot of land, yard and picket fence to separate them from their neighbors, defining mine as mine and yours as yours. Inherent to American suburbia is an emphasis on the pursuit of individual homeownership rather than a communal or corporate vision of civic identity. In fact, in the 1950s individualistic single-family houses were seen as the American antidote to communism. Communal housing was seen as a suspicious and dangerous step toward loss of individual identity and freedom. So suburban developers and architects encouraged individualistic homeownership as an expression of American freedom and one way to fight the Cold War.[16]

---

*"Unlike every other affluent civilization,
Americans have idealized the house and yard rather
than the model neighborhood or the ideal town."*

DOLORES HAYDEN, *BUILDING SUBURBIA*

The philosophical bent toward individualism and the commercial interests of the housing industries reinforce each other in an ongoing cycle. The more that individualism holds up "a home of your own" as the suburban American ideal, the more demand there is for single-family housing. The more single-family housing available, the more individualism, privatization and isolationism are perpetuated. Dolores Hayden observes, "The production of millions of houses—involving massive mortgage subsidies by the federal government, huge expense to individual families, and extraordinary profits for private real estate developers—has largely configured Americans' material wealth and indebtedness, as well as shaped American landscapes."[17]

The single-family house is firmly established as a universal ideal. While college dorm life or living with apartment roommates can have a fun appeal, we have a cultural sense that such shared living experiences should be a temporary phase before moving on to individual homeownership. Indeed, even the television show *Friends*, though extolling the joys of apartment dwelling in the city, ended its run by having its characters marry and move to the suburbs to raise their kids.

When we see advertisements extolling the virtues of owning your own home, we should ask ourselves, Who benefits? Whose economic interest is furthered by propagating this particular notion of the American dream? Why are banks quick to tell us that we can afford a larger loan and a bigger house, rather than smaller ones? Once we consider these underlying issues, we can begin to challenge the societal assumptions about what kind of housing we really need.

THE QUESTION OF SUBURBAN DIVERSITY

Suburbs now house half the American population, and this population is remarkably complex in terms of age, family status, income, ethnicity, and race. Individual suburbs, as is true with urban neighborhoods, are often homogenous, but suburbia as a whole is diverse. There is a mosaic of suburbs: upper-income, lower-working class, industrial, Hispanic, Black, Jewish, Republican, and mixed. In discussing suburbs and suburbanites, it is important to remember their complexity as well as their commonalities.

J. JOHN PALEN, *THE SUBURBS*

One of the biggest criticisms of suburbia is its relative racial, ethnic and socioeconomic homogeneity. It is commonly assumed that whites abandoned the cities and fled to the suburbs primarily to move away from minorities. Thus many see the creation of suburbia itself as inherently racist. While this story has a simplicity to it, the historical realities are a bit more complex.

Historians and sociologists still debate the causes, but it seems that postwar suburban growth predated the contemporary practice of "white flight." In other words, the primary cause of the postwar suburban boom was not because whites were moving away from black or minority neighbors who were moving in. Indeed, suburban growth patterns for the cities with small minority populations (like Minneapolis) looked the same as those for cities with large minority populations (like Chicago).[18] Suburbs grew to accommodate people coming back from the war and moving in from rural areas. The cities lacked adequate space to house all the new would-be metropolitan residents, so suburban housing developments exploded.

Furthermore, in the post-World War II baby boom suburban birthrates were higher than in urban areas, and ensuing generations of new suburbanites were suburban to begin with. While many urban centers have plateaued, suburbia has passed a tipping point where the demographic critical mass will continue to propel suburban expansion and self-propagation. Ironically, some urban-renewal efforts are drawing upscale whites back into the city but are pushing out the urban poor into older suburbs.

It is true that in many urban neighborhoods, as soon as ethnic minorities reached a particular percentage of the population, remaining whites quickly departed, whether to the suburbs or other urban communities. And some communities exercised subtle or overt pressure to prevent minorities from getting housing loans that would integrate neighborhoods.[19] But while racial issues certainly play a role in urban decay, race seems to be only one factor among many for suburban expansion. In fact, most new immigrants now locate in suburbs rather than cities. "The majority of Asian Americans, half of Hispanics, and 40 percent of American blacks now live in the burbs."[20] At the same time, the sheer number of white residents means that for all the growth in ethnic and racial minority populations, many suburbs are still largely white. Thus ethnic identity can be difficult to maintain in any sociologically significant way.

When my parents immigrated from Taiwan to the United States in the 1960s, they first gravitated to the urban metropolis of New York City. Many Taiwanese and Chinese newcomers likewise lived near urban Chinatowns or other communities with large ethnic Chinese populations. This critical mass meant that neighborhood institutions like stores and restaurants included many people of similar backgrounds speaking the same language·and maintaining their culture and ethnic identity.

But my parents moved from New York City to Minnesota, a state that is 95 percent white, predominantly Scandinavian and German, with an Asian American population of less than 2 percent. My experience growing up in the Minneapolis suburbs was certainly different than it would have been had I grown up in a southern Californian suburb where Asian Americans comprise a majority. While my family's presence in our Minneapolis suburb contributed some small degree of diversity to our neighborhood, in terms of overall sociological impact, our context affected us far more than we affected it.

As an ethnic minority, by no means do I mean to minimize the very real problems of racial injustice and the current socioeconomic disparities between cities and suburbs. While suburbs may have more diversity than expected, most are far from an equitable, cosmopolitan ideal. My neighborhood may have African American, Pakistani and Korean neighbors, but despite the ethnic and racial representation, all require a particular professional middle-class income and social status to live here.

Even so, there are signs that growing ethnic diversity and immigration patterns are changing how suburbs configure themselves. For example, suburbia tends to lack "street culture" or "street life," as social historians Baxandall and Ewen put it.[21] For many ethnic groups, street life is a trait of cultural traditions and heritage. But in suburbia, which lacks front porches and public gathering places, immigrant communities are frowned upon when groups gather on street corners. Such activities make predominantly white suburban residents nervous. Whereas the close proximity of urban neighborhoods makes block parties permissible and even natural, the privacy and insularity of suburbia discourages street life. One friend observed that when people move from the city to the suburbs, they set up lawn chairs on their driveways and actually talk to their neighbors.

Harkening back to frontier individualism, suburban homes are predominantly designed for single families, nuclear family units of parents and children. However, "suburban residents from different ethnic backgrounds have purchased older single-family houses and yards only to use them in new ways." For example, communities in suburban Fairfax County, Virginia, have many Vietnamese, Indian, Arab, Pakistani, West African, East African and Latino households with large, multigenerational families. "Their cars crowd small driveways. Dozens of these immigrant families have paved over their front lawns to make it easier to park, offending their neighbors."[22]

This example challenges Christians to consider what might be a more truly Christian way of living in suburbia. Immigrant families with multigenerational households, including aunts, uncles, cousins, grandparents and other relatives, demonstrate family values and identity not often seen in typical (white) American families, where relatives beyond the nuclear family rarely live under one roof. Middle Eastern, Latin American and Asian households actually have more in common with biblical examples of family, which were often large tribal clans.[23] Rather than asking immigrant families to conform to fragmented, isolationist Western models of suburban family life, it would be a collective benefit to our suburban status quos to be more accommodating to multigenerational extended families. Such healthy cultural diversity has the potential of invigorating our communities with more dynamic ways of civic and communal life.

THE QUESTION OF SOCIOECONOMIC HOMOGENEITY

Suburbs have always been physically, socially and culturally diverse, and will continue to become more so. I am optimistic and hopeful that differences of race, ethnicity and national origin are decreasingly significant factors in preventing people from living in most suburbs. I am more pessimistic, however, about increased diversity in terms of class and socioeconomic status. Suburbia is a commercial environment, and essentially, if you can pay, you can play. Access is largely limited to being able to afford the costs of living here, and as minority and immigrant populations continue to lag behind in income and wealth, they will continue to be underrepresented in suburbia.

Often people have limited freedom to choose their living environment. Many city dwellers lack the financial resources needed to live in suburbia, and many suburbanites find their choices restricted because they can't afford to live in particular costly suburban subdivisions. Thus there is a certain degree of economic and geographic determinism at work. Most of us make housing decisions thinking more about our financial limitations and constraints than any aesthetic or cultural preferences. Even if we would prefer to live in one neighborhood over another due to its local flavor or charm, we may find that we must settle for our second, third or eighth choice because housing costs are beyond our reach.

It's true that all areas have wealthier and poorer sections, whether in rural, urban or suburban areas. Class differentiation means that no matter the environment, the rich are not as likely to frequent a poor neighborhood and vice versa. But certain suburban communities formalize these distinctions through real-estate development and even local ordinances and laws. Exclusive gated communities physically prohibit undesirable economic classes from even visiting the neighborhood.

Sociologists note that suburban residential land-use patterns and housing valuations prevent many neighborhoods from having much variety of social and economic classes. Most subdivisions have a fairly narrow range of housing sizes and costs. As a result, if people want to move to a larger house, "the suburban pod system causes people to move not just from house to house but from community to community. Only in a traditionally organized neighborhood of varied incomes [such as pre-World War II urban communities] can a family significantly alter its housing without going very far. In the new suburbs, you can't move up without moving out."[24]

Of course, there can be exceptions to this. My supervisor, Andy, has lived on the same suburban block for three decades. In that time, as his family grew to include four children, he has lived in three different houses on the same street. They made a conscious decision to build an addition to their current house rather than move to a different community, because they wanted to maintain neighborhood presence and relationships. We can be intentional about finding ways to remain rooted in a particular local community rather than uprooting ourselves and relocating to entirely different areas.

The socioeconomic stratification of suburban neighborhoods often leads to a certain degree of local socioeconomic homogeneity, where residents are isolated and separated from those of different income brackets and backgrounds. Commentators have argued that the resulting psychological and worldview affect on suburban residents, especially children, is detrimental:

> A child growing up in such a homogenous environment is less likely
> to develop a sense of empathy for people from other walks of life and
> is ill prepared to live in a diverse society. The *other* becomes alien to

the child's experience, witnessed only through the sensationalizing eye of the television. The more homogenous and "safe" the environment, the less understanding there is of all that is different, and the less concern for the world beyond the subdivision walls.[25]

Anecdotally, it seems that this socioeconomic isolationism leads to suburban youth seeming overly sheltered and naive about global economic realities. When a school district's range of economic diversity only reaches from the middle class to the upper class, students have less understanding of what actual poverty looks like. I remember my high school classmates trying to figure out what it meant to be middle class. No one claimed to be either poor or rich; we all thought of ourselves as middle class, whether our parents made $50,000 a year or $250,000 a year.

Suburbia is often considered homogenous in ways other than race or socioeconomic status. The very layout and construction of suburbia is often critiqued as generic, all looking the same. I remember visiting some suburbs of Detroit, the capital of American industrial mass production, where identical postwar homes filled the landscape for miles on end, with little variation in house design or color. Movies like *The Stepford Wives* highlight how this kind of mass production seemingly eliminates any individual identity. Many post-World War II developments of tract housing were built with housing patterns that all look the same, with row after row of clone homes.

While many suburban subdivisions begin with cookie-cutter housing designs, such communities are not doomed to remain so homogenous. After the first wave of settlement, communities often naturally and organically mature and diversify. People of different ages and life situations move in and out, and houses are expanded or torn down and rebuilt. Residents bring their own creativity and individuality to their homes and personalize them to reflect their individual tastes.[26]

While homogeneity may give way to diversity, affordability can also give way to exclusivity. An irony is that many of the Levittowns built half a century ago are now too expensive for new residents. New York's Long Island, home to the first Levittown developments, now has a median single-family home price of $393,000, more than twice the national average.[27] This puts "starter housing" outside the reach of many young workers, who must search elsewhere for the affordable housing Levittown was intended to provide.

FROM LEVITTOWN TO CELEBRATION

Every generation has attempted to develop its own version of the ideal community. In the mid-1960s, Walt Disney had a vision for a futuristic city of twenty thousand people that would live beneath a giant dome and would travel between skyscrapers via high-speed monorail. There would be no slums and no unemployment. It was his vision of utopia. He dubbed it the Experimental Prototype Community of Tomorrow, or Epcot.

But Disney died in 1967, and his dreams of Epcot the utopian city died with him. The EPCOT theme park, which opened in 1982, retained little if any of Disney's original vision of an ideal residential community. It was not until the mid-1990s that The Walt Disney Company developed ten thousand acres of company land just south of the Disney World theme parks for residential housing. The town was named Celebration, and it was mapped out as a community for twenty thousand residents, just as in Walt's original dream.

Celebration was billed as the best that planned residential living could offer: upscale modern housing designed by world-class architects and visionary urban planners, and mixed-use areas, with main streets and downtown shopping integrated with housing and recreational space, all within walking distance. "There were to be commodious parks and civic spaces and closely set houses with inviting front porches to foster neighborliness, a sharp contrast to the isolation in most cities and suburbs these days. Everything would be an antidote to the creeping horrors of car-dominated suburbs."[28]

Paradoxically, whereas Disney's vision for Epcot was one of a futuristic Tomorrowland, the reality of Celebration became a nostalgic search for America's small-town past. Celebration was so highly hyped that it was impossible for reality to live up to utopian dreaming. Celebration's housing, marketed to upper-class middle-aged baby boomers, was significantly more expensive than comparable real estate in the Orlando area. Disney's target market for Celebration is the top 10 percent of the housing market. For all its idealism in creating a mixed-use, walkable community, it mostly imports affluent outsiders, not local residents.

Residents chafed under restrictions that controlled what colors and décor their houses could have or what plants and trees could be visible in their yards. The micromanaging tendencies of the Disney corporate powers made the reality of Celebration somewhat less than paradise. And being in the heart of Florida swampland, people tended to stay indoors after sunset because of advisories about encephalitis-bearing mosquitoes, putting a damper on front-porch community-building efforts. As some Celebration residents say, "The pixie dust wears off quickly here."

Despite hopes that Celebration's attractive downtown design would facilitate walking and render cars unnecessary, most residents still cling tenaciously to their automobiles. The "complex and persistent habits of daily auto dependence," it seems, are "a psychology that street planning alone would not alter easily." As commentator Alex Marshall notes, "The residents of Celebration are still utterly dependent on U.S. 192, and always will be. They drive there to shop for groceries. They drive to the Wal-Mart to buy some lawn furniture. They drive to the mall to buy a computer, a lamp, or almost anything essential."[29] And Celebration's walkable downtown can only survive if it brings in income from a larger region than its immediate neighborhood.

Planned communities like Celebration replicate old urban and small-town neighborhoods. The irony is that most urban and older suburban areas have plenty of existing neighborhoods that have the same environmental frameworks at a fraction of the price. "Why buy a thin, tepid version of what one supposedly desires at a far greater cost than the real thing? The answer says a lot about people's desire for control and to be controlled, and their fears of race and class," says Marshall.[30] It also exemplifies our consumer culture's emphasis on the new and improved. It feels easier to buy a new house in a new development than to refurbish an old house in an old neighborhood.

So rather than build an expensive new home in a planned community, why not buy a comparable home in an older community? Marshall notes that you could build twice the size of house in nearby Kissimmee for the same price as one in Celebration. But few Celebration residents are willing to move to Kissimmee to experience a real small-town environment. The lesson of Celebration is that *"people don't want to live in a real Florida small town! They want to live in a fake small town where they can pretend to live in a real one."*[31]

Celebration is not the only attempt to manufacture the perfect community. Another example is Seaside, Florida, a "neotraditional community" designed by architects Elizabeth Plater-Zyberk and Andres Duaney, founders of the Congress for a New Urbanism. Their approach was a reaction against the mass-produced postwar suburb that instead attempted to create mixed-use communities that encouraged civic interaction. These reactions to modern suburbia have themselves been critiqued as an unrealistic fantasy. "Seaside is a packaged collection of nostalgia from a past that never was—except perhaps on television."[32]

IN SEARCH OF CHRISTIAN SUBURBIA

> *[Today,] the very idea that gave birth to the mass-produced suburb—decent housing as a right for all—is seldom heard. . . . Private builders are more interested in building new communities for the upper middle class than providing suburban housing for the less affluent.*
> ROSALYN BAXANDALL AND ELIZABETH EWEN, *PICTURE WINDOWS*

Are there alternatives to Levittown on the one hand and Celebration or Seaside on the other? Columbia, Maryland, is a positive example. Columbia, started in 1967, was one of the first suburban communities to offer integrated housing. It is ethnically and racially diverse, with various kinds of housing, including single-family dwellings, apartments, town-houses, rentals, senior and single-person homes. It is connected to Washington, D.C., and Baltimore by public transportation. It remains accessible to people of varying socioeconomic incomes. But this kind of suburban intentionality is rare; indeed, many municipalities have zoning restrictions that prevent a neighborhood from having multiple kinds of housing affordable to different income brackets.

What happens when suburban housing costs increase beyond the reach of the average citizen? Newer developments need to be built far-ther out where land is cheaper, contributing to our commuter culture. What might it mean for us to work for affordable housing in suburbia? How could Christians help provide housing for people who can't afford the cost of living in suburbia? Imagine what could happen if Christians in local government and real estate, housing, and building industries marshaled their resources, in collaboration with local churches and parachurch ministries, to find ways to make suburban living less of an economic burden and more of a civic and communal joy.

As a practical matter we could begin by repudiating the notion that we *need* our own houses or that we should have as big a house as we'd like. Big houses are statements of class in America's supposedly "classless" so-ciety. "In 1950, the average single-family home was 983 square feet. By 1970, it was 1,500. Today it is 2,329."[33] American homes are by far the largest in the world. The typical American occupies a house with 718 square feet per person, compared to 442 square feet per person in Canada or just 170 square feet per person in Japan.[34] It is convicting to consider that the size of house we think we need for our families and children would actually house multiple families in other parts of the world. Dethroning Western individualism would help us discern what kind of housing is truly reasonable and appropriate for us. We could consider how single-family homes could be used in creative ways to house multiple households, thus sharing costs and increasing community.

We have difficulty even conceiving of alternatives to individualistic single-family housing. I once heard Christian futurist Tom Sine speak about the virtues and benefits of communal living and housing. He lamented that so many young Christians were taking on inordinately large mortgages in order to buy individualistic houses that they couldn't afford and that isolated them from community. He proposed that Christians pioneer alternate forms of housing, such as "sixplexes," where one housing unit holds six families. Each family has their own living quarters, but central to the complex is a large, shared kitchen, dining room and common area. That eliminates the redundancy of each family having their own appliances. Costs could be shared and reduced, children naturally play with one another, and communities can be multigenerational and include extended family.

Dan Chiras and Dave Wann of the Sustainable Suburbs Project describe how some communities have been pioneering what is called "cohousing." Local neighborhoods and community activists cast a vision for residents to remodel their existing suburban neighborhoods into communities with access to shared space and facilities, such as a common house. They remove fences between houses and create common areas for community gardens and orchards. While residents still have individual homes, they don't need to be as large and self-autonomous; some can be more affordable micro-homes with just a few rooms of private living space. The neighborhoods foster interaction and mutual support, such as babysitting co-ops, carpools and community entertainment. Such communities inventory their assets and share one another's lawn equipment, tools, vehicles and the like, reducing the cost of suburban living. When cars aren't needed, garages are converted into shared space or apartments, providing additional housing that is more affordable than single-family living.[35]

Various Christian organizations have created and championed intentional living communities in the inner city, and they have ministries of presence to their immediate neighborhoods. Similar communities could be established in suburbia. Just as urban churches have encouraged members to move into a particular neighborhood, so too have some suburban churches encouraged members to live strategically in particular suburban subdivisions, creating a critical mass of Christian residents who can have neighborhood presence, witness and influence in the local community.

We should also consider how Christian principles of hospitality and human dignity apply to our suburban context in regard to care for the poor, the alien and the refugee. A sign of the times is that Habitat for Humanity's work now takes place beyond the inner city and poor rural areas, becoming more prominent in suburban communities. As poverty becomes more pervasive in suburban areas, the need for Habitat-type inexpensive housing for people with low incomes is increasingly significant.

We might also consider that suburbia itself might be infused with Christian purpose and meaning. In eighteenth- and nineteenth-century Great Britain, for example, early suburban areas were intentional communities for families to have healthy environments for their children. They were conceived as places where green spaces and common civic areas were in close proximity to both residential housing and workplaces. Christian abolitionist and activist William Wilberforce helped establish one of these intentional suburban communities in the 1790s. About seventy people lived in and around Clapham Common, a housing development that purposely created "space in which discussion of public and private affairs took place in the company of spouse and children." Wilberforce's movement against the slave trade was organized and debated in this suburban setting. Women launched initiatives for their children's education and spiritual growth. "In other words," notes theologian Robert Banks, "suburbia was preeminently an evangelical creation!"[36]

Whatever kind of suburb we might live in and however we might construe our notion of the ideal suburban life, a more thoroughly Christian approach to suburbia will consider how the civic good can be advanced in light of the coming of the kingdom of God. For Christians, living in suburbia must be more than a private quest for the promised land or the good life. It also includes positive objectives like accessible, affordable housing for those without, and it embraces a larger vision for God's transformative work to be done in the community in relational, practical and spiritual ways.

As suburban Christians we can pray, "Thy kingdom come—to suburbia! Thy will be done—in suburbia!" We can envision a community where God's good shalom is experienced by residents and visitors alike. We can begin in the suburb where we reside, and pray for God's mustard seed of kingdom influence to take root and grow.

Spaced Out

The Impact of Commuter Culture

The city is doomed. We shall solve the city problem
by leaving the city.

Henry Ford

My wife, Ellen, and I live in Downers Grove, a suburb of Chicago. We both work at the same company, located in the adjacent suburb of Westmont, five miles away. Before we had kids, we were able to carpool together to the office, which was about a thirty minute roundtrip in normal suburban traffic. Not bad at all.

After the birth of our first son, Ellen shifted to a part-time schedule, working twenty hours a week. For Josiah's first year and a half, we alternated our time in the office so that one or the other of us was always at home with him. I would be at the office in the morning, go home at lunchtime and then work from home in the afternoon while Ellen was at the office. We were now making two roundtrips to the office each day, doubling our commuting time, but the upside was that we didn't need any outside childcare.

Then Ellen increased her work schedule to thirty hours a week. We were at home alternating mornings and both in the office every afternoon when Josiah would be at a sitter's. In the morning I would drive fifteen minutes to the office in one car. At lunchtime, Ellen would take Josiah in the other car to our sitter, who lived two suburbs away, ten miles in the opposite direction. This would take about twenty minutes. After dropping him off, it would take about half an hour to get to work. At the end of the workday, I would drive thirty or forty minutes to pick up Josiah and then another twenty minutes to get home. At the same time Ellen would be driving home to meet us for dinner. The next day, we'd switch, with Ellen in the office all day and me at home in the morning, taking Josiah to the sitter at noon.

In other words, what used to be a half-hour total commute in one car had become over two and a half hours commuting in two cars. We had effectively quintupled our commute. I remember idling in traffic one late afternoon, halfway through my forty-minute trip, thinking, *This is not the way it's supposed to be.* I wondered how God felt about all the wasted time and resources. Surely there was a better way.

According to the U.S. Census Bureau, the typical worker in America's metropolitan areas spends 24.4 minutes getting to work each day. This reflects a range from an average 16.5 minute commute in Wichita, Kansas, to a 38.4 minute commute in New York City. But anecdotally, these figures seem low. Many people commute forty-five minutes or an hour or more to work each way, heading for the office around six in the morning and not getting home until seven at night, leaving little time in the evenings for family, civic or church activities. It's not unusual for people to live two hours from their job, commuting over four hours every day.

Even those who don't commute to a city for work still commute. Many of us live in one suburb, shop in another and work in a third. We commute between several different kinds of suburban settings day in and day out. "We still think of commuting as going into the city in the morning and returning to the suburbs at night. However, in reality most commuting is from suburb to suburb."[1] As the book *Suburban Nation* puts it:

The first complaint one always hears about suburbia is the traffic congestion. . . . Why have suburban areas, with their height limits and low density of population, proved to be such a traffic nightmare? The first reason, and the obvious one, is that everyone is forced to drive. In modern suburbia, where pedestrians, bicycles, and public transportation are rarely an option, the average household currently generates thirteen car trips per day. Even if each trip is fairly short—and few are—that's a lot of time spent on the road, contributing to congestion.[2]

Suburban housing produces suburban commuting. The primary need of shelter creates the secondary need of access to and from that shelter. Suburban commuter culture is one of the most significant issues modern suburbanites face. How did we get here?

THE BEGINNINGS OF COMMUTER CULTURE

Early American cities were built in densely packed layouts patterned after medieval European cities.[3] Commercial, industrial, administrative and residential activity generally took place within walking distance. In the pre-Civil War era, the radius of even the largest cities did not extend over three miles. In preindustrial times, nearly everyone lived less than a mile from their place of work.[4] Homes and farms were largely places of production. It was not until the industrial revolution and the development of the modern factory that workers left their homes and commuted to work. Even then, by necessity many workplaces were within walking distance, simply because alternate modes of transportation were neither available nor affordable.

In the mid-nineteenth century, new transportation technologies began to give people increased mobility and geographic access. As early as the 1830s, public omnibuses, a type of large urban horse-drawn stagecoach, provided transportation for middle-class citizens who couldn't afford their own horse and carriage. Most major cities had dependable streetcar service by the 1860s.

The invention of the steam engine and the growth of the railroads introduced the possibility of commuter rail lines. At first railroads saw passengers as inconveniences, preferring to concentrate their industry on transporting cargo. After seeing the profitability of transporting commuters, cities established rail lines to bring residents in and out of center cities, to and from outlying smaller towns and embryonic suburbs. Because of their speed, smoothness and infrastructure, the railroads were the predominant form of travel away from home up until about the 1920s.

AUTO AUTOCRACY

By far the most significant transportation advance was the development of the automobile. While prototypes of horseless carriages had been invented as early as the 1860s, it was not until Henry Ford popularized the Model T that automobiles became affordable to the average citizen.[5] Cars were no longer a luxury limited to the elite. By the 1920s, "cars were being increasingly viewed as necessities . . . for those suburbanites not located near a rail or streetcar track, the auto was a commuting necessity."[6] The boom in automobile ownership stimulated a quantum leap in the building of roads and paving of streets.[7]

With roads increasingly in place, suburbs built for automobile commuters became a reality. Previously inaccessible areas could be developed for residential housing, which was in high demand due to population growth. "During the 1920s middle-class, auto-based suburbs sprang up surrounding every major city." Though development slowed during the Great Depression, by World War II, "the auto had become the prime means of suburbanites, and even many city dwellers, commuting to work."[8]

Then came the postwar development of the Interstate Highway System. Wanting to replicate the efficiency of the German autobahns for military purposes, the U.S. government passed the Interstate Highway Act of 1956 and created their own comparable highway system. The result was easy access to new suburban growth and development. "The roads afforded those who once had to live in a city and walk to work at a factory the chance to have a home in the relative safety, privacy, quiet, and cleanliness of the suburban countryside."[9] By the mid-twentieth century, suburbia as we know it had been firmly established as a car-based commuter culture.

More than any other invention, the automobile has completely altered how modern society lives and operates. Economies live and die because of the vast scale of the automotive industry, and wars are fought to ensure the flow of oil to fuel society's dependence on the car. Commercial real estate, malls and churches must factor in significant amounts of land use for parking lots. Besides its impact on housing and commerce, the car has also been responsible for disturbing levels of environmental pollution and millions of traffic deaths. The number of people who die in car accidents is the equivalent of two passenger airplanes crashing *every week*. What is it about the car that we deem beneficial enough to outweigh all its deadly side effects?

Quite simply, the car represents a convergence of personal independence, freedom, mobility and autonomy. Once made affordable, cars liberated their owners from the restrictions of train schedules and the annoyance of traveling with crowds of people. This lines up perfectly with American individualism and pioneer spirit, offering modern-day people a way to saddle up (on a Bronco, perhaps) and set out on their own frontiers. It's no mistake that car brands play into this with names like Explorer, Voyager, Blazer, Odyssey, Pathfinder and Expedition. Car drivers maintain an illusion of personal control over one's fate, even if travel patterns are largely determined by external forces.

In modern society, getting a driver's license at age sixteen is a more significant rite of passage than being able to vote at age eighteen. After all, in many ways a young person's life is far more practically changed by the ability to drive than the ability to vote. It represents the ability to direct one's own path, to not rely on others for transportation.[10]

Housing and transportation are usually the two largest expenses of modern life. They can also represent a dual idolatry. The location of a house determines the use of one's car, and the use of the car shapes how our lives are ordered and organized. We can find ourselves caught in a vicious cycle: our housing leads to our commuting, and our commuting is necessary to support our housing.

"People [base] their decisions on where to reside,
earn a living, shop, play and meet for worship
on the basis of the automobile."

ROBERT BANKS

In a suburban metropolis, the cost of housing pushes people to live and drive farther out and away from their workplaces. Marianne Hall commutes seventy-three miles each way from her home in DeKalb to her job in Chicago, spending four and a half hours on the road every day. The main reason for her location is that she is able to afford a much larger home in DeKalb than she could have for the same price closer in. Edward McMahon, senior resident fellow at the Urban Land Institute in Washington, D.C., says, "People keep driving farther out until they find a house they can afford."[11]

"I don't care how far I drive; I love my new house," said Betty Lou Wagner, who has a fifty-seven-mile commute to her job in Chicago. Of course, the irony is that those who have such lengthy commutes, spending two or three hours on the road each day, have little time to enjoy their houses. Such suburbs truly become bedroom communities, in that residents may not have much time at home to do anything except sleep.

Analysts note that for a new housing development to be successful, it generally needs to be within a thirty-five or forty-minute drive of significant job markets. This increasingly means intrasuburban commuting to other suburbs and exurbs, not to urban centers. One consultant estimates that commute times of sixty to seventy-five minutes are tolerable, "but at 90 minutes everything breaks down. Most people won't do it."[12]

In many ways the automobile has become a victim of its own success. Because the automotive industry has been so successful in making cars available and a necessity for every family, the sheer number of cars on the roads has strained infrastructure to the breaking point. Commute times and traffic gridlock continue to increase and contribute to frustration and road rage. Ironically, "Traffic congestion results in the construction of additional roadways, which encourage people to drive more, generating more traffic."[13]

The amount of time the average commuter now spends commuting, if consolidated, would be over three weeks a year. One car company attempted to give this data a positive spin. Its commercials for its luxury cars described the rich leather interior and climate-controlled comfort. They ask you to think of your time in the car not as a frustration of being stuck in traffic but as "a three-week vacation."

The amount of time per day that Americans spend . . .

- **watching TV or movies: 2 hours, 50 minutes**

- **in their car: 1 hour, 41 minutes**

- **in leisure-time physical activity: 19 minutes**

"STATS TO GET YOU MOVING,"
HEALTH, SEPTEMBER 2004

THE IMPACT OF COMMUTER CULTURE

While cars and commuter culture have been unquestionably helpful in terms of personal mobility, freedom and convenience, they have had tremendous unintended consequences and negative impact as well. The physical infrastructure of highways has had myriad and complex societal effects, especially for disadvantaged and minority communities.

The Interstate made long-distance commuting possible, thereby contributing to the "white flight" that separated races and classes from each other. More often than not, urban planners laid down the roadways in the neighborhoods of African Americans, Hispanics and other minorities, people who did not possess the political power to challenge them. In the ensuing years, planners and residents alike found that new highways had the power to divide rather than unite us, and that they could transform a once vibrant neighborhood into a cold, alien landscape.[14]

The cost of purchasing and maintaining automobiles is prohibitive for many low-income people, and limited resources are available for public transportation. Those who are unable to use cars, like many senior citizens, find themselves without access to areas that have been built with cars in mind. Retirement homes only came into being after the postwar suburban expansion, because sprawl created an environment where it became a necessity to drive everywhere. This inadvertently marginalized elderly who could no longer drive. Whereas in the past they may have still been able to walk to neighborhood shops, now they found themselves dependent on other people to drive them places, often making homeownership unsustainable.[15]

"In many places in America now, it is not actually possible to be a pedestrian, even if you want to be."

BILL BRYSON, *A WALK IN THE WOODS*

I am reminded of this whenever I see a middle-aged or elderly person carrying a bag or two of groceries, walking alongside the shoulder of a busy four- to six-lane thoroughfare. Because there are no sidewalks, they are dangerously close to the traffic. The environment was not designed for pedestrians, or even bicycles. These roads are for cars. And stores are located far enough from housing that it becomes nearly impossible to carry one's groceries or supplies home without a back seat or a trunk.

Most suburban environments, because they are planned for cars rather than pedestrians, are not very aesthetically pleasing. Environmental psychologist Albert Mehrabian points out that most New Yorkers walk far more than people in suburban Los Angeles. Manhattan residents think nothing of walking a mile to work precisely because the route is visually interesting to the pedestrian. On the contrary, to walk anywhere in Century City in west Los Angeles is a "long dull haul on foot" because people usually drive from one entertainment or shopping complex to another, and thus developers don't waste resources on such aesthetics as murals or art. People speed by too quickly to appreciate them.[16]

Commuter culture's most significant impact, perhaps, is on how suburban residents connect and relate to one another. Theologian Robert Banks observes:

> One of the key victims of the automobile is the experience of local neighborhood. Since people drive to and from their homes, they do not see, greet or talk with each other much anymore; since they go greater distances to shop and relax, the corner store disappears, and the neighborhood park empties, so removing the chief hubs of local neighborhood life.[17]

Ironically, residential suburbs solved one set of problems but created others. During the industrial era, many urban industrial communities were overcrowded slums without satisfactory sanitation or public works infrastructure. Workers and their families found themselves in dangerous conditions both at work and at home. By creating residential areas far away from industrial complexes, suburbs improved public health and decreased overcrowding and dangerous living conditions.[18] Fewer children grew up in the shadow of smokestacks, and many had more opportunities for play in open space and green areas.

So residential commuter suburbs began as a well-intended, positive effort to better workers' lives. But the unintended consequence of moving away from working districts was that suburban living eroded the sense of neighborhood community. Since workers no longer walked to work neither did children walk to school or homemakers walk to the corner store. Now everybody drives everywhere. The urban jungle has been supplanted by the suburban commuter culture.

Sociologist Robert Putnam, in his landmark study *Bowling Alone,* traced the decline of community in modern America since the mid-twentieth century. His thesis is that society's "social capital" has been eroding, with fewer people gathering in such organizations as Rotary clubs, Boy Scouts, bowling leagues or church groups. The decline of social capital is not primarily due to the transience of people moving, since residential mobility has actually stabilized and even declined in recent decades. Contributing to the breakdown of community are various time pressures and family changes, but significantly Putnam singles out suburban commuter geography: "Suburban sprawl that has fractured the spatial integrity of our lives is a surprisingly important contributor."[19]

Putnam argues that there is a direct correlation between commuting and community—the more commuting, the less community. "The car and the commute are demonstrably bad for community life. In round numbers the evidence suggests that *each additional ten minutes in daily commuting time cuts involvement in community affairs by 10 percent.*"[20]

Suburban commuter culture diffuses our personal relationships and connections over a wide geographic area. We don't work in our local community. We don't make friends in our neighborhood. We commute elsewhere to shop, to study, to worship. Our friends Dave and Kara told us that any time they wanted to get together with friends from their megachurch, they'd have to drive forty-five minutes to an hour. Some people commute to Willow Creek Community Church in the Chicago suburbs from the neighboring states of Wisconsin or Indiana.

Furthermore, the layout of suburban areas has affected our physical health. Recent medical studies have shown that the more sprawling and spread out a suburb, the increased incidence of obesity, high blood pressure and weight-related chronic illnesses, precisely because we walk less and drive more. "Cities encourage walking and physical fitness, the authors argue, whereas suburban homes are so far from friends, stores, and workplaces that even the most health-conscious residents are forced off the sidewalk and behind the wheel."[21]

Shortly after this report was released, a local newspaper article looked at health and fitness practices of suburban residents. It described one man who exercises regularly by running several miles at a nearby forest preserve. Though the park entrance is only six blocks away, he still drives his car to get there. Why? Because the physical layout of the area has made the preserve virtually inaccessible to pedestrians. There are no sidewalks to or from it, and major roads surrounding it are too busy to cross on foot.

SUBURBS MAKE YOU FAT

"Americans are walking less than ever, but not necessarily because they're lazy, say health experts. It's because they can't. There are no sidewalks nearby, the school is miles away, and a six-lane highway separates home and stores."

THE WEEK, MAY 9, 2003

A study in the journal *Public Health* reported that suburbanites had significantly higher rates of lung disease, migraine or chronic severe headaches, arthritis, abdominal complaints and bladder problems. Besides the lack of physical activity, the study also cited air pollution from cars as contributing to lung diseases, asthma and headaches.[22] Suburbs were created to escape the public health dangers of overcrowded urban industrial districts, but their very geography and layout have created new health risks of their own.

COUNTERING COMMUTER CULTURE

It is no easy matter to counteract the tyranny of the commuter culture. It's not as simplistic a solution as "live closer to your job" or "work from home." Our employment choices may well be quite limited; certain careers may only have a few possibilities open to us, and we may find it impossible to leave a company or find a new job. Many suburban Christians still have long commutes even after relocating to be closer to their workplaces. Many couples find that their jobs are located many miles apart from each other, and even living midway means that both spouses still drive a half-hour or hour to work. This creates more complications in that neither parent may be nearby a child's school in event of emergency. Some dual-income families make intentional choices to live directly by one spouse's job, even if that means that the other must have a lengthy commute, so that at least one parent can be closer to home.

Each of us has a certain threshold of tolerance for commuting, and that will naturally vary from person to person. I'm not willing to drive two hours to work, but someone else might be. Our life stage and family situation will determine how much time we are willing to spend on the road. And many of us eventually come up against situations where we become convinced of the need to change our lifestyle and commute patterns.

At the beginning of this chapter I mentioned that what used to be a half-hour commute for me and my wife had quintupled to over two and a half hours commuting in two cars. The increase in our monthly gas expenses had become noticeable, especially as this was during a time of conflict in the Middle East and oil prices were high. We realized that our new schedule had eaten away the advantage of living close to work. Our commute was the same as that of coworkers who lived an hour away. We wanted to reclaim some of that time to decrease the commute, save gas and spend more time together as a family. What could we do?

Our options were fairly straightforward. We could change our childcare, change our work situation or change our housing. Of these three we prioritized our workplace as the most important to us and the least likely option for changing, as we both enjoy our jobs, appreciate the benefits of working in the same company and feel a sense of calling to our work. So we ruled out changing our work fairly quickly.

Our family was growing, so we looked for new housing and considered finding a house nearer to work. We looked at some townhouses very conveniently located just a few blocks from our office, but they were way out of our price range, over double the cost of our current home. On the other hand, we could have moved further out to the newer development where our sitter lived, where we could have had a much larger house for the money. In fact, the house next door to our sitter's was for sale, and it was tempting to imagine living there. But it was half an hour further away, and we decided that a shorter commute was a higher priority for us than more living space.

After several frustrating weeks of exploring housing possibilities hither and yon over a range of suburbs, we happened to notice a house in our neighborhood was for sale. We looked into it, and it lined up well with what we were looking for: a modest increase in space to accommodate our growing family, at a price we could afford. And it was just two blocks away from our current home. Having lived in Downers Grove for several years now, we wanted to continue to have a sense of rootedness in this community. So we bought that house and moved two blocks closer to work. We are able to walk to the same park, see the same ducks, continue shopping at the same local stores and use the same public library.

What was most significant in reducing our commuting was changing our childcare arrangements. As it happened, our sitter's husband took a new job, and their family moved away from the area. A colleague recommended a childcare center close to our office, which we now use a few days a week, and the rest of the time we alternate working from home and having my mother over for childcare. Though we now have the additional complexity of another child, we are mostly down to an hour-long combined roundtrip commute.

Different families may well make different choices, depending on their situations and priorities. Some may find it easier to quit their job and find a new one or start their own business. Others might be able to find affordable housing near their work. Whatever your situation, consider ways to minimize your commute. As a rule of thumb, it's usually physically, emotionally and spiritually healthier to spend less time driving to and fro.

RECOVERING A PARISH MINDSET

The concept of the local parish offers an alternative to modern commuter culture. Many small towns and older urban communities were often understood in terms of the local Catholic parishes, even by those who were not Catholic. Such communities often have a more tightly defined sense of space, and in some places people are able to live, work, go to school, shop and worship all within a few blocks. Most suburban settings have geographic land-use patterns that fight against this local sense of neighborhood parish, but we can still ask ourselves what it might look like to do as much locally as possible.

Think of what happens to us when we live, work and worship in different communities. If we live in suburb A but work half an hour away in suburb B and commute twenty minutes in the opposite direction to a church in suburb C, we find our sense of identity fragmented. We are *dis*-integrated, and our loyalties and connections are diffused into three different geographic areas. We especially feel tension and dissonance when driving from one area to another, say from a church function in one community to a school event in another. There is little overlap between our disparate worlds.

On the other hand, consider the benefit to us when we live, work and worship all in the same community. Then we have triple the sense of investment and rootedness, and we increase the potential for overlap between neighbors, coworkers and fellow church members. Instead of feeling pulled apart in three different directions, we rather have a sense of wholeness and re-integration. Identification with a particular community wards off the fragmentation of commuter culture.

Pastor Randy Frazee, author of *The Connecting Church*, suggests:

> Scope out a one-mile radius around your home. . . . Seek to do as much within this radius as possible. Shop in this zone; send your children to schools there. Most important, concentrate the development of your Christian community within this circle.[23]

For some of us, a one-mile radius won't even take us out of our own subdivision and may not get us to the nearest grocery store, but whatever the actual scale or distance, Frazee's concept has merit. I tend to think in terms of a roughly square area of about five miles across that includes my own suburb as well as parts of those immediately adjacent. The vast majority of my activity in any given week takes place within this area. My workplace, the library, the post office, the gas station, the grocery store, my favorite used-book stores and comic book shop are all within this zone. This is my "parish."

Of course, this doesn't mean that I ignore the world outside my parish. Plenty of places lie outside this area, including our church and many of our friends' homes. And I certainly don't walk everywhere in this zone; sadly, I even find myself driving between the library and the post office, even though they are just two blocks apart. But this parish concept is a step toward reintegration. I am spending most of my time within five miles rather than ten or twenty. Most tellingly, in times of crisis or emergency, we find ourselves calling on friends that live within this area. Others are simply too far away.

Not only is it helpful to invest in a particular geographic *area,* it is also important to invest a significant amount of *time* there. Usually the longer we can stay in a local community, the better. St. Benedict asked new members of his monastic communities to take a "vow of stability" rather than to wander constantly from place to place.[24] Many suburbanites move every few years, thus preventing them from investing deeply into a local community. Moving to a new home just two blocks away was a conscious effort on our part to practice a spiritual discipline of stability, to stay in an area and call it our own rather than move somewhere else and start all over. Stability allows us to invest more in our local parish and build the relationships needed to have a healthy sense of community.

---

*"To be rooted is perhaps the most important and
least recognized need of the human soul."*

SIMONE WEIL

What is your parish? What would it look like for you to invest most of your activity and relationships in your local geographic area? Consider how your commuting patterns could be changed to counter fragmentation and recover a sense of parish.

PRACTICAL STEPS

When all is said and done, most of us will still find ourselves commuting a lot. And many of us do what we can to redeem that time, whether using it for devotional prayer or listening to audio books. Those who commute on public transportation are able to read the paper or books or get work done on laptops. Ken Taylor, founder of Tyndale House Publishers, paraphrased what would become the Living Bible during years of daily commuting on the train from Wheaton to Chicago. We can all find practical ways to counteract the negative aspects of commuter culture. The following is certainly not exhaustive, but here are a few ideas.

First, as a matter of personal fitness and health, we should consciously try to drive less and walk more. If something is within a mile, try walking instead of driving. If something isn't within walking distance, instead of driving all the way to a destination, drive for part of the trip and then walk the rest of the way. Don't always try to find the closest parking space. Park at the far edges of the lot. The walk will be good for you, and your car is less likely to be dinged.

But won't this take longer? Isn't walking inefficient? Won't this waste precious time? Perhaps, but too often contemporary Christians have been held captive by modernist notions of efficiency. We try to be more efficient and economical with our time. We get restless when Sunday morning services last longer than an hour. Little do we realize that the whole notion of thinking in terms of hours and half-hour segments is a purely modern notion developed with the advent of clocks and timepieces, and we are primarily inculturated into this measured regime by the dominance of television shows.

Efficiency is an industrial value, and not necessarily a Christian one. Yes, the Scriptures warn against sloth. But efficiency is not held up as an ultimate virtue. Many Christians today are rediscovering a "holy inefficiency," in which relationships and longitudinal time take priority over accomplishing tasks quickly and expediently. As John Ortberg was told by a mentor, "You must ruthlessly eliminate hurry from your life."[25] There is something profoundly countercultural about walking to the park while cars speed by on the thoroughfare.

It's not surprising that the Gospels describe many instances where Jesus is walking with his disciples. We never hear of Jesus speeding along in a chariot. On Palm Sunday he rode a donkey, but we sense that the donkey walked at a normal gait, not a gallop. We don't imagine Jesus powerwalking through Galilee, as if he were some speedy urbanite with things to do and places to go. The more natural picture is one of Jesus strolling along at a leisurely pace, chatting with his disciples, considering the lilies of the field. While he may have set his face toward Jerusalem and walked purposefully, his attitude was not one of hurrying from one appointment to the next.

During recent controversies about gasoline consumption and sport utility vehicles, some organizations asked the question, "What would Jesus drive?" Inherent in that question is an assumption that Jesus would drive at all or own a car. Isn't it more likely that Jesus would walk? Or take public transportation? If suburban commuter culture has so imprinted itself on our ways of life that we can't imagine life without a car, then Jesus would challenge our imagination.

The questions of "What would Jesus drive?" and whether or not Christians should drive SUVs are somewhat misguided. As Eric Jacobsen points out, he could own a gas-guzzling SUV and still consume less fuel than someone with a more fuel-efficient hybrid car. Why? Because Jacobsen lives in a mixed-use neighborhood and mostly walks everywhere while the other car owner might commute an hour and a half each day to work. Geography and commuting patterns are at least as important as fuel efficiency, if not more so.[26]

We need to remind ourselves that it's okay that walking takes longer than driving. It takes me far longer to walk to the park with my son than to drive there and back, but along the way he notices things that we don't see when we speed by at forty-five miles per hour. He points out letters etched into the concrete or squirrels scurrying up trees or bunnies hopping by. The qualitative experience is both slower and better.

Walking also allows us to do things that we can't do while driving. While walking through our neighborhood, we came across a shopping cart from the local store that had been abandoned alongside the road. I decided to push the cart back to the store. It was less than a mile away, and the roundtrip took me the better part of an hour, but this was a civic good that I couldn't have done had I driven past the cart in my car. It is much harder for potential good Samaritans to help people in need when zipping past them on the freeway than it is to stop by when you are on a neighborhood walk or jog.

Pastor David Hansen, in his book *Long Wandering Prayer*, reminds us of the benefits of literally walking with God. He talks about the spiritual value of walking physically as we pray, that we will see things and pray about things that come to mind in ways that don't occur when we are sitting solitarily at home. "In long wandering prayer the mind wanders through topics as the body wanders through woods, streets or church halls."[27] Many Christians are rediscovering the spiritual practice of prayerwalking. As we walk through our neighborhoods, we can pray for the people who live in the homes, the children who go to the schools or whatever God shows us to pray for. Step by step, literally, he leads us.

Not surprisingly, walking more will also reap physical benefits to our health.[28] In the three and a half years between the births of our two sons, I lost about twenty pounds. As far as I can tell this didn't happen because of any significant change in diet. The main lifestyle changes were chasing a preschooler and taking more frequent walks to the park.

Get a pedometer to measure your walking. Fitness advisers suggest walking ten thousand steps a day, but most of us do only five thousand or less. Find out how many steps you walk on average, and then look for ways to increase that. Not only will this help you maintain your physical health, it can also be an opportunity to cultivate solitude with God when walking alone or building friendships when walking with others.

Finally, see if you can decrease your dependence on your car by bicycling, using public transportation or carpooling. According to the 2000 census, 87.9 percent of Americans drove to work, 4.7 percent took public transportation, 2.9 percent walked, and 0.4 percent biked. The vast majority of commuters, 75.7 percent or three out of four, drove alone to work. Only 12.2 percent carpooled.[29]

At my own workplace, growth in number of employees has meant that our parking lot is reaching capacity, with quite a few people parking on side streets. But our need for parking spaces could be alleviated if more of us carpooled. It can be inconvenient, but we benefit from opportunities for friendships as well as savings and stewardship of resources. It also puts us at the mercy of someone else's schedule and vehicle. It dethrones us from our own autonomy. This is not a bad thing.

I heard a story about a journalist who consistently came up with fascinating, award-winning human interest stories. Her editor asked her how she kept on finding such interesting people. She said, "Simple. I ride the bus." By taking public transit, she was able to meet people she wouldn't otherwise connect with were she in the isolation of her car. She eavesdropped on conversations and got a sense for what ordinary people were thinking about. Taking public transportation can also show us the limitations and challenges that others face, when infrastructure and systems are not helpful for getting people to work, school or church.

Sometimes the only time we consider alternatives to driving is when we have car trouble. Once when both our cars needed repairs, our three-year-old son, Josiah, picked up on my frustration and said, "The car is broken? It's okay, Papa. We can walk." When a car is in the shop, we are forced to consider what life is like for those without them. Of course, many of us have multiple cars, so to have one out of commission is a minor annoyance at best. But as a spiritual discipline, try to live without a vehicle for a week, or use only one car instead of two. Fast from driving. (Should that be "slow"?) Force yourself to consider alternative modes of transportation. Carpool with others to work or church. Yes, it will take more time. Yes, it will be somewhat inconvenient. But it will conserve gas and enhance your relationships. It teaches us interdependence and trims back our sense of self-sufficiency. And you may discover that you may be able to get by with fewer vehicles than you currently own, or none at all.

We forget that cars are not necessities and that the vast majority of human history got along fine without them. While Revelation's picture of the New Jerusalem is undeniably an urban city environment, nobody ever speaks of driving there. We always look forward to *walking* on those streets of gold.

MATERIAL WORLD

The Challenges of Consumer Culture

Simply put, the suburbs—where houses have on average doubled
in size and miles driven annually has tripled since the 1950s—are
the best possible invention for mindless consumption.

DAN CHIRAS AND DAVE WANN, *SUPERBIA!*

This may be a vast oversimplification, but if rural areas have been primarily agricultural and urban areas have been primarily industrial, suburban areas have been primarily commercial. While all people in every environment need to purchase goods for everyday life, consumption is an integral dimension to suburban geography and identity. As one scholar puts it, "Suburban culture is a consuming culture. Fueled by the increasing commoditization of everyday life, suburbia has become the crucible of a shopping economy. There is an intimate and indissoluble link between suburbia and buying."[1]

Numerous books have been written about consumerism, and I can't possibly unpack everything that could be said about it. But this and the next chapter will offer a few observations about how consumer culture works and consumption's sway over suburban Christians, with some ideas toward countering its influence in our lives.

SUBURBAN HOUSING AND CONSUMER CULTURE

The very housing structures of suburbia itself contribute to consumer culture because of the primacy of the single-family home. Rather than the homestead being a place of production, the single-family home is a place of consumption, necessarily fueled by wages to support a consumption-centered lifestyle.[2]

As automobiles distanced us from extended family, single-family homes forced nuclear families to become more autonomous rather than reliant on shared family- or community-based production. Instead of labor being done by relatives, it's done by appliances or hired workers. While the single-family home is symbolic of American individualism and frontier independence, ironically, its very location in an atomized, suburban context makes us ever more dependent on commodities and consumption.

It would be nearly impossible for average suburbanites to produce milk and eggs from their own cows and chickens. It is far more cost-effective for professional farmers to have the cows and chickens. Even though fabric is readily available, it is seldom that people sew their own clothing, let alone spin their own thread. It is far easier to buy a T-shirt than to make one.

The single-family home, because it is dependent on consumption for its continued existence, "ensures the endless perpetuation of consumer desire."[3] The single family, says Miller,

> is socially isolated and particularly vulnerable to instabilities in income. This is a particularly cash-intensive form of life, which makes it difficult for extended family members and friends to support one another in times of crisis. Former acts of communal support such as barn raising or providing labor to run a farm or business are difficult to reproduce in the contemporary setting.[4]

One of the ironies of modern consumerism is that much of the burden of the work is placed on the consumer rather than the retailer or shopkeeper. The average fast-food restaurant actually provides very little in the way of customer service. Customers are expected to bring their own food to their tables, get their own refills and throw away their own trash. Half a century ago doctors made house calls and the milkman personally delivered fresh milk as regularly as necessary. Today, in contrast, consumers must go to the grocery store themselves to procure goods. The only remaining regular home delivery of a product is the daily newspaper. Indeed, Internet grocery delivery services like Peapod have something of a retro-nostalgic feel of harkening back to the days of home delivery.

Of course, we cannot easily revert to an agrarian, communal society of extended, multigenerational families with homesteads of shared production and provision. For better or for worse, we live in a postindustrial consumer society. If consumption is inescapable, are there ways to moderate or mitigate our consumption? Is there any way to consume more Christianly?

CONSUMERISM AS IDEOLOGY AND WAY OF LIFE

The late Pope John Paul II critiqued consumerism as "no less pernicious" than the evils of racism, Marxism, Nazism and fascism. He described consumerism as an ideology where "the selfish satisfaction of personal aspirations" becomes the ultimate goal of life.[5] Consumerism becomes a false god, an alternate religion. But all of us consume in order to live. How did we get here?

The problem lies in the larger systemic forces of consumer culture. Modern consumer culture has made it virtually impossible to do anything but consume. Most of us have jobs that segment out one particular task or area of production or service. Since we cannot easily barter our work as dry cleaners or accountants to obtain oil changes or spaghetti sauce, we now have money as the common unit of commerce and trade. We are paid monetary wages for our work, and we use that money to pay for the fruit of other people's work. This is simply how the world works today, and it is certainly far more efficient and productive than a barter economy.

Thus it is nearly impossible for any one of us to *create* rather than *consume* or *purchase* any of the items we use and rely on in daily life. Light bulbs, toaster ovens, computers, even items as simple as chairs or tables—the best I can do is put things together that have "some assembly required." I have no idea how a car engine works, or a CD player or a digital camera. I could never manufacture any of these items on my own, so I instead become a purchaser and consumer of them. Someone else does the actual making for me.

All of this has changed our acquisition of goods into financial transactions rather than exchanges of mutual relationships. We no longer have real embodied relationships with the people or communities that produce the items we purchase. The modern economic system depersonalizes all of the participants in the process.

Therein lies the rub. In other eras of history, production and consumption took place locally, and only one or two links separated the farmer from the market, the carpenter from the neighbor buying his wares. But as modern consumers in a consumer society, we rarely see or know how the goods we consume are made. Commodification of products distances us from their local communities or origins. We don't know if a fruit or vegetable was farmed with dangerous pesticides or if a pair of jeans was made in a sweatshop by child labor. Now production is so far removed from consumption that consumers make their purchases with no knowledge of the context or human cost of their consumption.

Vincent Miller tells the story of a nineteen-year-old Chinese woman named Li Chunmei who worked in a toy factory near Hong Kong. She was a "runner," taking partially completed stuffed animals from one work station to another, working from eight in the morning to midnight, on her feet all day with only two hours of break time for meals. She earned twelve cents an hour. She tried to rest one evening, skipping a mandatory overtime session, and was docked three days' pay as a result. Chunmei worked for sixty days straight, seven days a week, until she collapsed and died from exhaustion.

"As I see this story in the newspaper," Miller writes, "I force myself to read it, to regard the photographs of an unhappy young Chinese woman. A voiceless knot of grief forms in my throat. Did Chunmei work on any of the animals I am tripping over this morning?"[6]

It is nearly impossible for Miller to know. In our consumer culture the only thing in view to us is whether the products we consume benefit *us*. The unintended consequences on others in the labor and supply chain are invisible to us and largely ignored. As Pope John Paul II put it, in the ideology and system of consumerism any resulting "negative effects on others are considered completely irrelevant."[7]

CONSCIENTIOUS CONSUMPTION

Consumer commodification enthrones us—the consumer—and makes everything a function of our choosing. It's a particular notion of the self. Our self-understanding is that we determine what we will consume. However, while we usually think of ourselves as choosing between various goods, many choices have already been made for us. Product developers, market researchers and industry gatekeepers give us certain kinds of products to consume and not others. In many cases, no matter what we choose to consume, we cause unintended consequences on local communities.

Even so, if we as consumers knew that our toys and sweatshirts were being created by a permanent underclass enslaved by industrial exploitation, we'd think twice about what we purchase. Imagine if every item on the store shelf, rather than being labeled by price and sale stickers, instead had pictures of the people who made them and information about whether the purchase helps them or hurts them. Then we might be less concerned about how the item benefits us and more concerned about what effect our purchases are having.

A starting point is a greater mindfulness about our consumer choices. A book like *Fast Food Nation* or a movie like *Super Size Me* will open our eyes to the realities behind the hamburgers and kids' meals. Rather than seeing them as inexpensive fast food, we might begin to think about the larger complexities at work to deliver the food to us so cheaply. A book like *Nickel and Dimed* or *The Wal-Mart Effect* will make us consider the possible negative side effects of shopping at discount retailers that may exploit their workers. We can consider shopping at local farmers' markets or family-owned stores or restaurants to bypass some of the depersonalized structures and reconnect with actual producers and suppliers.

We won't be able to grasp all the dynamics at work behind every item we purchase, so Miller suggests that we identify one item that we especially connect with and research its origins so we can make informed consumer choices about that particular item. He gives the example of bananas. Most of us give little thought to bananas apart from how many are in a bunch and how green or yellow they are. But different countries have different practices for producing bananas. For example, Ecuador in particular has few protections for their labor force, and workers are routinely exploited, meaning that bananas from Ecuador are exported at lower costs than those from other countries. "When such details are considered, bananas are no longer generic commodities. They are reconnected to their context."[8]

After reading Miller's example, the next time I went to the grocery store I looked at the bananas and looked closely at the little "Chiquita" stickers on the bunches. I discovered that they mention the country of origin; in this particular case, Guatemala. It was the first time that I had consciously thought about bananas as originating from a local community and not just as a consumer choice.

I also realized that making informed consumer choices one item at a time has a cumulative effect. I now know something about bananas; I add that to what I already know about fair trade coffee. As we continue to learn more about different kinds of items, we begin to have a larger, more cohesive perspective about the overall socioeconomic ecosystem. Things interrelate, and the combined knowledge helps us make better decisions about how to consume more wisely.

We can also seek out patterns of consumption that help local communities rather than hurt them. A few suburbs away from us is a store called Ten Thousand Villages, a ministry of the Mennonite church.[9] It sells handcraft items and goods made by people in Two-Thirds World nations, and the economics are such that a more equitable amount of income goes directly to the individuals and communities that make the goods rather than corporate or industrial intermediaries. This enables them to make a living and move out of poverty. Buying Christmas presents from Ten Thousand Villages is a step away from ordinary consumerism toward conscientious consumption.

CONSUMING LOCALLY

I grew up in Minnesota, home to the Target Corporation and birthplace of Target retail stores. In my youth, Target was a local chain, and I thought of Target as embodying Minnesotan values and style. I didn't realize that Target had already begun expanding across the country. When I came to Illinois for graduate school, I was thrilled to find a Target not too far from me. When I was homesick for Minnesota, I went to Target. The layout of the store in suburban Chicago was much the same as the layout of the store in suburban Minneapolis. It reminded me of home.

In recent years Target has had great success in becoming a nationwide chain. I still have tremendous loyalty to Target and prefer to shop there rather than at other comparable retailers. But I realize now that for most Target shoppers, Target says nothing to them about Minnesota. It is simply another place to shop. For the most part, it has lost its local and regional connotations. In becoming a major national chain, it has lost its sense of place.

Local versions of national chains still have some neighborhood flavor, if only by virtue of the fact that they hire local employees. But shopping at national chains and big-box stores tends to take money out of a local community. Studies show that chains return an average of 13 to 14 percent of dollars spent in their stores to local economies, and much of the rest departs to the national office and suppliers. On the other hand, locally owned, independent stores recirculate 45 to 58 percent of their dollars to the local community.[10]

In my local suburb's downtown area, there's an independent ice cream store called Every Day's a Sundae. As far as I know, this is the only one of its kind anywhere on the planet. Locally owned and managed, it employs teens from the community and provides a tip jar on the counter for college funds. While I am probably helping local teenagers earn college money no matter where I get my ice cream, something about Every Day's a Sundae's homegrown ethos reminds me that this store, its employees and patrons are all rooted in a particular community.

I think also of the Tivoli Theatre, a playhouse in downtown Downers Grove built in the 1920s and now restored as a second-run movie theater. On weekends someone comes and plays the theater's organ before movie showings. When the organist plays familiar songs, the gathering crowd takes on the communal feel of a concert audience. It provides a shared public experience. In some small way the Tivoli organist reminds me that I am not just a consumer of motion pictures—I am a member of a civic community.

My wife and I have long had a habit of going out to eat with friends after church. We once drew up a list of all the restaurants we could think of within a few miles. We came up with thirty or forty, and we decided to rotate more intentionally through the list. After a while we realized how our eating habits could better benefit the local economy if we went to independently owned restaurants rather than national chains. It's been fun to discover new restaurants, often hole-in-the-wall establishments in out-of-the-way places because they can't afford the high costs of prime real estate. While we still eat at national chains like T.G.I. Friday's and Bennigan's, we try to make a point of eating at local restaurants like Uncle Bub's and Moondance Diner.

COUNTERING CONSUMERIST IDEOLOGY

> *Consumer culture makes us constantly*
> *aware of what we do not have.*
> AARON FREEMAN, IN A COMMENTARY FOR
> NATIONAL PUBLIC RADIO

Consumer culture is a self-perpetuating phenomenon. The abundance of goods creates a class of consumers who work to afford to consume, which generates more demand for more goods, which creates more consumers. And on it goes.

Commentator Rodney Clapp writes, "Unique to modern capitalism and consumerism are the idealization and constant encouragement of insatiability—the deification of dissatisfaction."[11] Our economy depends on people in a constant state of needing more and wanting more, leading us to buy things we do not need. It's one thing for us to consume a mocha latte on occasion, but it's quite another for us to be seduced into a daily habit of cappuccino consumption. The subtlety of consumer culture is that ordinary, everyday good things become commodified and marketed to us so that one is not enough. It's not merely the individual purchase that the consumer economy is after; it's the cultivation of the habitual, repeat buyer who comes accustomed and acculturated to a pattern of consumption. Consumer culture wants to create addicts.

Advertisers do not "simply cater to preexisting needs but create new needs."[12] For example, in the early days of toothpaste, Colgate used advertising to teach people the need to brush one's teeth daily. "Diamond engagement rings are not a time-honored tradition but a product of re-

cent vintage, brought to us by—who else—the diamond manufacturer."[13] Now the diamond industry is marketing the concept of diamond rings for women's right hands, to enlarge their market beyond
engagement and wedding rings. The ad campaign declares, "Your left
hand says, 'I love you.' Your right hand says, 'I love me, too.' Women of
the world, raise your right hand." Nobody *needs* a diamond ring on the
right hand. This is a purely artificial need, created by an industry to sell
more of their merchandise.

We can counter some of the effects of consumer culture by guarding
against such marketing messages. Richard Foster says, "We need to greet
with sarcastic laughter all those patently phony television commercials.
In unison the family should shout, 'Who do you think you are kidding!' "[14]
Better yet, mute or skip commercials entirely. Avoid sponsored shows
with intrusive product placements. Recycle advertising circulars from
the Sunday newspaper without reading them; resist the temptation to
look through mail-order catalogs. Juliet Schor says that we must "rein in
desire . . . stay away from malls and upscale shops, knowing that such
exposure inevitably creates desire."[15]

A side effect of suburban abundance is the temptation toward a sense
of entitlement. The lines between necessity and luxury become blurred.
We can't imagine life without a microwave oven. Even if we don't have
the latest high-end plasma screen television, we already have far more
luxury items than most people throughout history or around the world.
Children growing up in the suburbs may have a distorted sense of what
the average family "needs" to own.

On the other hand, having kids can be a good reminder of the transience and impermanence of our stuff. I have resigned myself to the likelihood that sooner or later, my kids will get their hands on some of my
rare, autographed, out-of-print books and will scribble on them and tear
them apart. I am expecting this to happen so that it does not surprise me
when it does. While I will do what I can to protect my belongings from

NINE PRINCIPLES FOR COUNTERING CONSUMERISM

1. *Control desire: Avoid things that make you want more.*

2. *Create a new consumer symbolism: Ignore luxury branding messages.*

3. *Control ourselves: Participate in community efforts to reduce consumption.*

4. *Learn to share: Both a borrower and a lender be.*

5. *Deconstruct the commercial system: Become an educated consumer.*

6. *Avoid "retail therapy": Don't shop to make yourself feel better.*

7. *Decommercialize rituals and holidays: Find alternatives to gift-buying.*

8. *Make more time to spend less: Downshift your lifestyle.*

9. *Support civic and government efforts to limit consumption.*

ADAPTED FROM JULIET SCHOR, *THE OVERSPENT AMERICAN*

undue abuse, I will hold them loosely so that I am not entirely bent out of shape when something gets wrecked.

Of course, this is easier said than done. Shortly after I had these thoughts, my son poured a glass of milk on the keyboard of our laptop computer and killed it. The laptop completely shorted out and could not be rebooted. I had not transferred my files from the hard drive to a floppy disk. All the data was lost. I was tremendously frustrated and raged and pouted for a while, but I realized that this was exactly the kind of thing I should have been preparing myself for.

We can loosen the hold that possessions have on us by relinquishing them to the reality that everything we own will eventually pass away. Whether in our lifetime or afterward, all our prized possessions will someday become useless junk. Moreover, the very commodification of consumer products makes these items replaceable. If you lose or break something, fear not, for a manufacturer will be eager to sell you another one. If the replacement cost is prohibitive, we may need to go without. And then we may discover that we don't really need it after all.

Whenever we consider what we would rescue from our homes in the event of a fire, we invariably list the things that are not mass-produced commodities. Family heirlooms and old photo albums, a grand-mother's quilt or a child's homemade art project—these are the things that have value, precisely because they can't be picked up at the mall. The paradox is that "the priceless things in our life are likely to have no monetary value."[16]

CONSUMER CULTURE VERSUS CHRISTIAN PRACTICE

Cultural commentator Andy Crouch suggests that there is a big difference between consumer culture and Christian practice. He cites a Starbucks advertising slogan to "Live More Musically." This is something that most people could nod their heads to. Yes, we should be more musical, more melodic, more artistic. Who would disagree?

But Crouch points out the vast difference between how this slogan is understood by a *listener* of music and a *practitioner* of music. For the casual listener, living more musically means turning on the radio or buying a CD. It's an act of consumption, and a mostly passive one at that. But for the musician, living more musically means practicing at one's instrument and honing one's craft. As Crouch writes:

> There is a big difference between playing a CD and playing a fugue. One is instantly rewarding, the other takes time and patience. One satisfies, the other requires a sacrifice. One is godlike—Yo-Yo Ma or Radiohead play flawlessly at your command—while the other reminds you just how small a creature you are. One is a purchase, the other is a practice.[17]

Practice goes further than consumption. Someone might listen to jazz, blues or hip-hop CDs as a way of appreciating African American culture and experience. But it's another thing entirely to locate ourselves in communities where crossracial relationships and reconciliation can take place.[18]

Consumer culture means that we are shaped by our purchases. But Christian faith calls for us to be shaped by our practices. And perhaps too much of our Christian culture is shaped by Christian consumerism. Christian paraphernalia does not necessarily a Christian life make. Beyond being Christian consumers, we must also be Christian practitioners as well.

What this means is that we must practice the historic spiritual disciplines that Christians have practiced throughout the ages. One in particular is the discipline of fasting. Not just fasting from food, though many of us would do well to practice that regularly. Fasting as a rhythm of relinquishment reminds us that our desires don't always need to be sated. Indeed, for many Christians around the world, hunger is not alleviated. Fasting from food puts us in voluntary solidarity with those around the world who don't have what we too often take for granted, and can prompt us to pray on their behalf, "Give them this day their daily bread."

Fasting as a discipline can and ought to be extended beyond food to areas such as fasting from media, from new technology, new clothes or new products. It offers us an opportunity to say no. One youth pastor told me about how he was teaching kids in his youth group to fast, and they told him that they were surprised to discover how often they wanted something they didn't need. The discipline of fasting made them reevaluate every desire, every hunger pang, every prompting for something. And it taught them that not only *could* they say no to things, that they *would* say no to things.

Here's a diagnostic. How can people tell that I'm a Christian? Is it only by observing the Christian books on my shelf, Christian art on the walls, Christian music in the CD player, Christian stations preset on my radio and a Jesus fish on the back of the car? Or can someone observe my Christian faith through my practice of generosity? Are my words filled with grace and truth? Is my life evidencing a heart of peace, contentment, love and joy? Are my actions filled with compassion and mercy?

Am I an active member of a worshiping community, living out a life of service, ministry and social justice?

While all these things are hard for any of us to live up to, the goal should be that of inner and outward coherence and Christlikeness, where our inner spirituality matches our external activities and priorities. What that looks like for each of us will vary depending on our specific circumstances, personality traits and calling in life. But the key will be for us to practice our faith in ways that are distinctive and recognizable. And the more we invest our lives in Christian practices, disciplines and acts of service, we may find that we are consuming less.

To counteract suburban consumerism, I offer three main alternatives. We need to reclaim the Christian spiritual practices of creativity, simplicity and generosity.

CREATIVITY

> *Many a philosopher and theologian has stated*
> *that we most resemble the divine when we create.*
> VINITA HAMPTON WRIGHT, *THE SOUL TELLS A STORY*

The opposite of consumption is production. It takes far more time and energy to create something than to consume something. It takes a novelist a year to write a book that someone can read in a few days. A cast and crew of thousands spend years to create a film that will be viewed in two hours. Often our only recreational activities are actions of consumption. What an alternative it is, then, to rediscover the wonder and delight of creativity.

The very first dimension of God's character revealed in Genesis is creativity. God creates. It is who he is and what he does. This aspect of God's identity as Creator is likely one of the primary meanings of being created in the image of God. God is Creator, and we too are creators. Not in quite the same way, of course, since we do not speak worlds into existence out of nothingness. But we form and reform and shape and make things out of the world around us. We are created to create. As songwriter Michael Card notes, our creative efforts, performed in the presence of God in obedience to his call to creativity, are forms of worship.[19]

Andy Crouch notes that Christians have had a number of different stances toward culture. We have condemned culture as evil, and we have avoided culture. We have critiqued culture, and we have also tended to copy culture in our Christian subculture. Mostly we consume culture. But all of this is a far cry from God's intent, that we fulfill the creative mandate and exercise our energies to *create* culture.[20]

I took piano lessons for much of my elementary school years and hated practicing. It was painful, arduous work. But in high school and college I rediscovered the joy of making music. Some of my most joyful times are spent at the piano, playing familiar songs as expressions of worship, or doodling and making up my own melodies and progressions. I'm no composer, and much of what emerges from the piano would never be suitable for other people's ears, but in the process of making music I am tapping into a creative impulse that is fundamental to my human identity. I am recovering something of the image of God within me.

All of us have different ways that we express our creativity; all of us can be makers of one thing or another. To do needlework or to crochet a sweater, to craft with wood or to restore antiques, to program a computer or to plan a worship service are all creative actions that help us recapture some of God's divine intent for human existence. It's one thing to passively watch a sporting event on television and entirely another to organize and play a softball game in the neighborhood park. Instead of watching a movie, join a community theater production.

At times my wife will be stamping homemade greeting cards while my son is building things with blocks or drawing with crayons, and I'll be writing on the computer, giving form and shape to abstract thoughts.

Though creativity may require commodities that are in some sense consumed, whether card stock or toys or a laptop, we do not consume for the sake of consumption. We are exercising various capacities for creativity, and it's remarkable how invigorating and satisfying this can be. Creating may be exhilarating or challenging, but it's rarely boring.

The next time you go shopping, ask yourself if any commodities that you purchase could instead be homemade. Rather than buying greeting cards or thank-you notes, help your children design their own. Think of one or two areas of interest to you where consuming can be replaced with creating. As God leads you to exercise your creative gifts, you may sense the joy he intended for us to experience in the midst of human creativity.

GENEROSITY

> *Too often our possessions possess us, and a sure way*
> *to master our belongings is to give them away.*
> David Matzko McCarthy, *The Good Life*

I once heard a story about the late Christian musician and songwriter Rich Mullins. Every year or so he would go through his closet and look through his clothes. He'd sort them between those that were nice and those that were a little too worn, those that he'd like to keep and those that he'd rather give away. Then he'd give away the nice clothes and keep the grubby ones. It was his way of keeping material possessions from having too much of a hold on him. It was an exercise of the spiritual discipline of generosity.

Generosity, at its most basic form, is giving things away, divesting oneself of possessions or money for the benefit of others. Sometimes giving is cast in selfish, consumerist terms—give to this ministry and God will bless you tenfold. These crass motivational ways of soliciting only reinforce the self-centeredness of consumer Christianity. Generosity can become merely a tool for self-improvement.

But done honestly, selfless generosity does in fact benefit the giver. The spiritual discipline of generosity frees us from the power of greed and acquisitiveness. It reminds us that our resources are not our own. It is a subversive, countercultural practice that releases us from the bondage of consumer culture. Richard Foster says that every once in a while, we should look through our belongings to see what objects we most cling to, what has us in its grip. And we should then give them away.[21]

A loose hold on material possessions has been a Christian ideal since the earliest days of the church. In the New Testament, sharing was intrinsic to the church in the concept of "mutual aid, regarding possessions not as ours but God's gifts at the disposal of fellow Christians and the needy in general, and regarding ourselves as stewards, to distribute these material goods as God's Spirit directs."[22] Since God is spirit, we tend to lose sight of God when we cling to materiality. But even though God is spiritual, God's gifts are both spiritual and material, and are intended to be shared with others.[23]

I am a book geek, and one of my greatest joys in life is hunting for out-of-print books at thrift shops and used-book stores. Our house is cluttered with hundreds of books and overflowing bookshelves. My wife and I have this repartee that we say back and forth: one of us will sigh, "We have too many books," and the other will reply, "You can never have too many books, just not enough bookshelves." When I hunt for books, the demons of greed, materialism and book lust cackle overhead. At times it becomes an unhealthy, compulsive addiction, where I feel that I must own every book that strikes my fancy.

I eventually realized that I was acquiring far more books than I could ever read. Even when I would read a hundred or more books a year, I would collect hundreds more than that. There was simply no way I would ever catch up. My shelves were filled with dozens of books that I had never cracked open. I'd have twenty books on my nightstand, each with a bookmark stuck a few chapters into it, and I'd realize that the book on the bottom of the stack had been sitting there for two or three years.

So one of the best things that happened to me was to become our church's librarian. Instead of focusing on acquiring books for myself, as a church librarian I found myself hunting for books for others. I learned to look at books less in terms of how it would benefit me and more in light of how it might benefit someone else. I also began to cling to my own books less tightly. I learned to refute the materialist lie that says I need to personally own every book I find worthwhile. After all, I will never refer to the vast majority of my books more than once or twice. Far better that those books be accessible to others than sit on my own shelves unread.

So I donated several hundred of my own books to the church library, since it would be better for them to be in circulation among a Christian community where they could edify others. Giving them away was an act of generosity that mitigated my greed and book gluttony. I've also become more ruthless in regularly weeding out my own shelves. Instead of buying more bookshelves to accommodate more books, I now try to keep the shelving constant and give away books to make room for new ones. As a result, the house is less cluttered and my wife is happier.

My idea of heaven is the scene in Disney's *Beauty and the Beast* when the Beast takes Belle into the library, where there are books, books and more books in every direction as far as the eye can see. C. S. Lewis said that the books we lend or give away are the ones that will be in our libraries in heaven.[24] Perhaps giving away books is a way of storing up treasures above, where moth and rust will not destroy.

All of us have areas of acquisitiveness that need to be tempered by generosity, whether it's antiques or DVDs, shoes or mutual funds. What can you divest yourself of, for someone else's benefit as well as your own? What has such a claim on your soul that you simply need to get rid of it? Practice the discipline of generosity, above and beyond normal tithing and giving, and you may find that consumer culture has less hold on you.

SIMPLICITY

There are two ways to get enough: one is
to continue to accumulate more and more.
The other is to desire less.

G. K. CHESTERTON

It has become trendy in recent years to speak of simplifying our lives and living more simply. In the Christian tradition simplicity is putting possessions in proper perspective. Richard Foster calls it a "life of joyful unconcern for possessions."[25] It is repudiating the power of the false god of Mammon. It is an inner state of contentedness, gratitude and freedom from anxiety, exhibited in outward expressions of economic stewardship and lifestyle transformation.

While house hunting, my wife and I looked at a townhouse nearby our workplace. It was a very stylish place, brightly lit and well-decorated with fashionable, upscale furnishings. I sensed that the sellers had a standard of living and level of income several notches above ours. Indeed, the house was at least a hundred thousand dollars beyond our price range. But the clearest sign that this house was not for us was found in the garage. When I peeked in, I saw that the current owners had a Mercedes and a BMW. My wife and I own Honda and Chrysler minivans. If living in this neighborhood required an income that could afford two luxury cars, then we were clearly not going to be able to live here.

I say this as someone who has never owned a luxury car. Certainly there are plenty of suburban Christians who can easily afford and own such cars. And in global perspective many would see our two used minivans as luxuries. So what is appropriate "simple living" in a suburban consumer culture?

One rule of thumb is to try to live at a standard of living that is below others in your income bracket. If you can afford a $400,000 house, live in a $250,000 one instead. Or, if you can afford a $250,000 house, live in a $150,000 one. Even if you can afford a Mercedes, choose to drive a Honda. Our culture drives us toward ever more conspicuous consumption and tells us to acquire above and beyond what we can afford. As a Christian spiritual discipline of simplicity, we can try to live below and under what we can afford. The more we exercise self-discipline and voluntary simplicity, the more resources we will have available with which we can practice generosity.

In the Garden of Eden Adam and Eve took and ate fruit that was not only forbidden, but unnecessary, given the abundance of other resources at their fingertips. In our consumer culture, we are not so much tempted by forbidden fruit as we are tempted by *unnecessary* fruit. One pathway to simplicity is to evaluate our consumer choices through the lens, "Is it necessary for me to own this item?"

A significant change in my family's lifestyle was the discovery that we could get virtually any book or movie through our public library's interlibrary loan system. We have essentially stopped buying new books and renting new movies. If we hear of a new book or DVD that sounds interesting to us, we'll go online to our library's website and reserve it. With interlibrary loan, a requested item may not come in for several weeks or months, but we have learned that this is okay. What's the big hurry? Most of the time, it is simply not necessary for us to read a particular book or see a particular movie right now. Every item we get through the library is one fewer item purchased and cluttering our home.

There are myriad ways to live out simplicity. We have chosen not to have cable TV, since we rarely watch television and our house's antenna reception suffices. Others might eschew Internet access or cell phones. All of us have different criteria for what we might deem unnecessary. For some, it might be brand-name clothing. For others, it might be electronic and computer equipment. This is an individual discernment process that will necessarily be particular to your own situation and God's leading in your life. Simplicity is not simplistic. There are no easy answers or one-size-fits-all approaches to simple living. Simplicity is ultimately a spiritual discipline to be practiced in response to the calling and leading of God.

TEN GUIDELINES FOR PRACTICING SIMPLICITY

1. *Buy things for their usefulness rather than their status.*

2. *Reject anything that is producing an addiction in you.*

3. *Develop a habit of giving things away.*

4. *Refuse to be propagandized by the custodians of modern gadgetry.*

5. *Learn to enjoy things without owning them.*

6. *Develop a deeper appreciation for God's creation.*

7. *Be skeptical of all "buy now, pay later" schemes.*

8. *Obey Jesus' instructions about plain, honest speech.*

9. *Reject anything that breeds the oppression of others.*

10. *Shun anything that distracts you from seeking first the kingdom of God.*

FROM RICHARD J. FOSTER, *CELEBRATION OF DISCIPLINE*

Suburban living is fraught with consumerist temptations, but the more we practice such disciplines as creativity, generosity and simplicity, the more we will rediscover the joy and freedom of living in the material world. Our consumer culture has claimed material goods to be the ultimate goods, but by recalibrating our desires and practices, we can be freed from the tyranny of consumption and instead delight in things the way God intended, receiving them gratefully as gifts from his hand.

STATUS CHECK

How Consuming and Branding Shape Our Identity

America has double the number of shopping malls
as it does high schools.

LINDA KULMAN, *U.S. NEWS & WORLD REPORT*

It's a blustery spring afternoon in Chicagoland. I'm helping my mother pick up some furniture she has just purchased. We drive south from her home to the adjacent suburb, one that's on the outermost edges of the metropolitan area. Though I've been in this suburb before, I've not been in this particular community. Signs heralding new development line the main thoroughfare—"Single family homes from the $230s!" "New homes in the $190s!" This is the farthest out I've traveled in this direction, and open fields of farmland still exist here beside the newest subdivisions. I wonder how long it will be until those farms are developed into housing.

We pass through a new commercial zone where large retailers line the corridor. The Home Depot. Borders. Linens & Things. Closer to the farms, large swaths of land have been cleared for construction. It's obvious where the parking lots will go, and signs mark the retail centers that will be coming soon. The restaurants are the first to stake their claims, some already open: Red Lobster. Pizza Hut. The Olive Garden.

Though I've never been to this particular area before, there is something all too familiar about it. The vibe is largely the same as the suburb to the north or the suburb to the east. I have seen these land-use patterns before, even if this is my first time driving these streets. Though the community is new, the retail and commercial template is recognizable as having been used time and time again.

Then a somewhat obvious thought strikes me: The stores are all national chains.

As I look at the signage of what's there and what's coming, I see nothing that I haven't seen before. Starbucks. Verizon. Wendy's. Blockbuster. Walgreens. Everything new here is actually old, from national and multinational giants with long-standing brand identities. The only places with regional or local identities are the banks, and even those are extensions of larger conglomerates. Nothing has come from this actual locality. The only store name indicating any place of origin is Boston Market.

There are no new mom and pop start-ups here, nothing indigenous to this local community. There can't be, not in this retail environment. The space is too expensive for anything but the tried-and-true commercial brands that will automatically draw customers. The residents here are all transplants, and they bring with them their preexisting brand loyalties and affinities. So the retailers likewise come along, bringing to this community the familiar products and same shopping environments that the residents have experienced elsewhere.

In other words, commercial forces militate against the emergence of distinct and unique communities. This is why James Howard Kunstler calls suburbia "the geography of nowhere."[1] Particularity has been lost because of the powers of mass culture. Little distinguishes one suburb from another because larger commercial realities all but require everything to be basically the same as everywhere else.

Suburban consumer culture becomes all the more imposing because giant corporations, mall developers and brand retailers have invested billions of dollars into cultivating the suburban shopper. They play into our universal human longings for identity and community in order to create brand loyalty. They appeal to our vanity and desire for status in order to reap commercial profits. The challenge for Christians living in this consuming environment is for our Christian identity to determine our consumption rather than for consumption to determine our identity.

THE CALL OF THE MALL

Growing up in the suburbs of Minneapolis, I spent many weekend afternoons during my junior high and high school years at a local shopping center one suburb north of my hometown. Little did I know that my local hangout was a historic place. Southdale Center opened in 1956 in Edina, Minnesota, as the first fully enclosed, climate-controlled indoor shopping center in the United States. Outdoor shopping boulevards and strip malls had been built elsewhere, especially in warmer climates, but Southdale was developed in part because of Minnesota's harsh winters. An early press release proclaimed, "No matter what the weatherman says, it's always Spring at Southdale."[2]

Shopping malls are indigenous to the suburban environment, and the genesis of Southdale is representative of many suburban malls. After World War II, Minneapolis department store Dayton's realized that it could no longer focus all its energies on its downtown location. It needed to go where their customers were living, in the suburbs. As a result, Dayton's looked west to the growing village of Edina, believing that "there is no conflict between downtown and the suburbs—that it is the downtown merchant's responsibility to develop both."[3]

When Southdale was built, the land was a farmer's field. It became 800,000 square feet of retail space and 45 acres of parking. By the developers' estimates, Minnesota only had an average of 126 "really comfortable shopping days" a year, due to subzero winters and sweltering summers. By contrast, Southdale offered a year-round shopping experience "untroubled by soot, snow or wilting heat."

As the mall was developed, the two main anchor department stores, Dayton's and Donaldson's, negotiated to ensure that both stores would get equal exposure and foot traffic. At the time, it was revolutionary to have two competing department stores operating under the same roof.

Southdale was billed as "the first shopping center to plan a blight-proof neighborhood around itself."[4] The larger plan for developing the area around Southdale included a medical center, movie theaters, office space, even some residential living. It was thought that the mall would reduce car travel by consolidating multiple shopping destinations. The mall became an opportunity for suburban residents, primarily house-wives, to not only do their shopping, but also have access to banking, a post office, beauty salons, restaurants and entertainment for children, all in one convenient place. "Southdale's creator envisioned the center as a gathering place for the community. Southdale hosted gem, boat and fine art shows as well as serving as host for charity galas, community events and even an episode of the nationally known 'Truth or Consequences' game show."[5]

The mall included a garden court decorated with original artwork and sculpture, meant to evoke the sense of a European market square. Live birds, tropical plants, exotic trees from Africa, Australia and Asia, and fountains were part of the décor, meant to replicate the outdoors in an indoor environment. Southdale's architect, Victor Gruen, said, "By bringing the outdoors indoors . . . we are creating a new kind of environment—one of Eternal Spring—which provides a psychological and visual contrast and relief from indoor shops."[6]

> Whether sitting on a rest bench or at a table off the sidewalk café, the shopper finds pleasant eye-catching features all about him; brightly plumed song birds, art objects, decorative lighting, foun-tains, tropical plants, trees and flowers. They quicken the human impulse to mingle, and create an atmosphere of leisure, excitement

and intimacy similar to the one which can be found in some European city market squares.[7]

There's something distinctly optimistic and utopian about this vision of mall culture. Artificial nature, imported art and culture, in a human-controlled environment, promoting a comfortable suburban ideal without the hassles of weather change. If suburban life is a spiritual quest, we can interpret the building of suburban shopping malls as an attempt to create an earthly paradise. The Garden of Eden meets the New Jerusalem, with the advantages of convenient parking and food courts.

Southdale quickly became a model for other malls in the Minneapolis area—Rosedale, Brookdale, Ridgedale—as well as other shopping centers across the continent. It is fitting that the Mall of America, the largest of America's shopping centers, was built just one suburb away from Southdale, in my hometown of Bloomington. The Mall of America, known locally as the megamall, was built with enough steel to build two Eiffel Towers and enough concrete to lay a highway from Bloomington to Duluth, two hundred miles away. Two parking ramps hold 13,500 cars each. At peak times, like the day after Thanksgiving, the megamall holds some 150,000 people within its walls, almost double the population of the city around it. The megamall houses over four hundred stores, more than twice the number of many malls. The specialty stores in its opening seasons included one that sold only framed, preserved butterflies and another with only holograms. Shopping at the megamall can feel like visiting an art gallery, a science museum and an amusement park all at the same time.

But malls have fallen on hard times. In an era of online convenience, the cost of physical retail space is far too high for many stores to remain profitable as foot traffic plateaus and declines. Many malls hide empty stores behind signage and disguised construction barriers to provide the illusion of busy commerce and growth. Even marquee malls like the Mall of America have tremendous turnover, with stores failing constantly.

Ironically, mall culture not only creates consumers; the cost of retail itself consumes its own businesses and leaseholders.

When I go back to visit Minnesota now, I no longer have a home church. However, I still have a home mall—Southdale. I feel strangely at home there. Even though it has been remodeled and expanded and many of the stores are different, I still have nostalgic memories of hanging out there with my junior high friends. It is part of my sense of place. Despite its commercial nature, it is part of my suburban identity.

"Shopping malls are temples of trade, churches of consumption, synagogues of excess, or mosques of the market."

JON PAHL, *SHOPPING MALLS AND OTHER SACRED SPACES*

Historians say that you can tell what a culture values by studying its architecture. Coliseums, pyramids, cathedrals, monuments and skyscrapers all reflect ideal visions of what is most treasured. It is telling that some of the largest and most valuable real-estate properties in modern society are shopping malls dedicated to the sale of commercial goods. As one commentator observes:

> Suburbs are now being built around the mall, spatially defined by a symbolic and material dependence on what many have suggested are the cathedrals of our time. All the available variety and difference of late capitalism is displayed beneath dome and atrium, as fountains and fig trees, marble and glass, elevators and escalators, respectively contain, decorate and facilitate the endlessly effortless movement between nature and culture, heaven and hell. Shopping. Shopping.[8]

Shopping malls are a commercialized, privatized version of what used to be the public square.[9] Civic spaces in downtown areas have been disappearing, and shopping centers and big-box stores have both contributed to the decline of locally owned retail and have consciously set themselves up as alternatives to public gathering places. Whereas town squares used to be a common ground for government, commerce, community and cultural events, and even religious gatherings, malls elevate the commercial above all else. Shopping centers, quite naturally, make shopping central. If malls are our cathedrals, then consumerism is our religion and consumption is our gospel.

CONSUMER BRANDING

A recent ad for the Mall of America pictures dozens of signs from its stores: Macy's, Nordstrom, Pottery Barn, Abercrombie & Fitch, Ikea, Banana Republic, Apple, Godiva, J. Crew, Williams-Sonoma, Guess, Rainforest Cafe and dozens more. Most are widely recognized national and international brands; only one, the Twin City Grill, seems to be a local establishment. The ad doesn't actually depict any of these stores' products. There are no articles of clothing, electronics, furniture or chocolates. Just the names of the companies. The brand names themselves are evidently all that we need to know, because it is assumed that we know what these brands represent and that the names themselves will attract us to shopping there. In fact, what the ad is selling is not the brands' products but the brands themselves.

Branding is not an exclusively suburban issue; it shapes all of late-modern capitalist society. But if we suburbanites are by nature immersed in consumer culture, then we are especially affected by branding.

Suburbia has been described as a place of "competitive self-advancement and self-fulfillment," where "community counts for less and status and success for more."[10] If this is the case, then suburban residents are particularly tempted to accomplish more, achieve more and acquire more. While most of us would not consciously say that we're doing this to impress our neighbors or to keep up with the Joneses, there is often a subtle dynamic where we purchase something not because of its functionality or workmanship but because of what statement the item will make about our own success and status. We are hyperaware of what our neighbors might think of us, even if we never meet them.

Affluence and socioeconomic success have always been markers for class status, and in today's consumer culture, having products with desirable brand identities is a convenient way of achieving such status. In some societies, class is permanently assigned on the basis of caste or an aristocratic hierarchy. In a consumer culture, however, we can attain the image of a higher social class by purchasing the correct brands to identify us as part of the societal elite. Americans are particularly luxury and brand conscious because the United States lacked the aristocratic class and status markers of Europe. Status is now conferred by material possessions rather than titles of nobility.

Branding is about status and identity. It signals something to the outside world if the logo on your car is a Mercedes-Benz or a Lexus instead of a Chevrolet or a Kia. Or if you wear clothes from Ann Taylor rather than Kmart, drink Starbucks coffee rather than Folgers, or buy groceries at Whole Foods Market rather than Safeway. James Twitchell, author of *Branded Nation,* says, "I grew up in a world where social place was well defined at birth. People cared if you were Jewish or Catholic and about the tint of your skin." Today, however, "in this new 'brand world,' we make judgments about people based on their consumption."[11]

Brand awareness begins at a very early age, almost immediately. When our second child was born, he was given a baby Ralph Lauren outfit, complete with the hallmark Polo logo on the chest. According to Boston College economist Juliet Schor, author of *The Overspent American,* children recognize logos by age eighteen months.[12] I was startled when my two-year-old looked out the car window, pointed at the golden arches and said, "Madonald's. Frensh fries."

The average American child sees some forty thousand commercials a year.[13] The American Psychological Association says that before the age of four or five, kids can't distinguish between shows and commercials. The American Academy of Pediatrics is on record saying that it "believes advertising directed toward children is inherently deceptive and exploits children under age 8."[14]

In 1984, the Federal Trade Commission deregulated children's television and allowed TV shows and toys to be developed and marketed together. Prior to that, television shows were watched without cross-merchandising ancillary products; there were no *Leave It to Beaver* action figures or *Gilligan's Island* Lego sets. Many of today's Gen X adults nostalgically remember the cartoons of the mid-1980s—*Rainbow Brite, Strawberry Shortcake, My Little Pony, Care Bears, Transformers* and *G.I. Joe*—all of which were essentially half-hour commercials for their respective products. Nine of the top ten bestselling toys of that era were tied to TV shows.[15] Now we can't imagine TV shows without product families and collectible items. Older television phenomena, like the late-1970s *Schoolhouse Rock!* segments, have been retroactively developed into new products to be marketed to today's young adults—even though there were no consumer products based on them when they originally appeared.

Schor's research demonstrates that "higher consumer involvement by children can lead to depression, anxiety, low self-esteem, more psychosomatic complaints, and worse relationships with parents." Her "Survey on Children, Media, and Consumer Culture" shows that kids steeped in consumerism are more likely to get depressed. "It teaches kids to measure themselves by asking, 'How much do I have, relative to other people?'"[16]

The simplest response would be to unplug the television, or at least to limit programming that is tied to commercial products. But even educational shows like *Sesame Street* or *Blue's Clues* have been branded so kids shop for Dora the Explorer backpacks and The Wiggles pajamas. What are we to do when our toddlers express preference for one brand of diaper over another simply because Elmo appears on them? Our son Josiah went through a phase where he only wanted Shrek-shaped fruit snacks, even though he had never seen a Shrek movie. Even Christian media entities practice commodification and brand extension—VeggieTales characters Bob the Tomato and Larry the Cucumber can be found on bandages, party favors and greeting cards, not to mention neckties, throw pillows, coloring books and even veggie-shaped chicken nuggets.

Ellen and I had heard that *Blue's Clues* was an intelligent and engaging educational program, so we checked out a few videos from the library. Josiah loved them, and we were suitably impressed with the educational content that we started buying the videos (used, off of eBay). Little did we realize how quickly this would lead to brand loyalty and increased consumption.[17] When we did a quick inventory around our house, we were staggered by the realization that not only have we collected over twenty Blue's Clues videos and DVDs, but Josiah also has Blue's Clues books, CD-ROMs, pajamas, T-shirts, toys, sippy cups, dishes, bedsheets and pillowcase, Halloween costume, fruit snacks, toothpaste, toothbrush, backpack, board game, and handy-dandy notebook. It's not that our son demands these things and we just cave—it's the more subtle reality that when buying everyday items, our family now has a predisposition toward buying the Blue's Clues brand. If Josiah needs a toothbrush, we think that he will be more likely to brush his teeth if he has a Blue's Clues toothbrush than a Buzz Lightyear one. For many children's products, unbranded, generic versions often aren't even available.

Such branding and consuming is by no means limited to children. Indeed, our childhood habits train us to be brand-conscious adults. Adults are equally susceptible to buying an unneeded article of clothing or coffee mug simply because it sports the logo of a particular name brand, a favorite football team or movie franchise. Monopoly board game editions are tailored for fans of Star Wars, NASCAR, Lord of the Rings, Justice League, The Simpsons and dozens more. Anybody who has ever browsed Disney's emporiums at their theme parks knows there is no end to the possible products that can be branded. One shopping complex in Orlando is the equivalent of an entire mall that has been Disney-fied; stores have Mickey Mouse tablecloths and plate settings, jewelry and curtains, with mouse-ear-shaped pasta, chocolate, spoon rests, and bath soap.

The impact of childhood branding and advertising is long-term. Edward Hallowell, author of *The Childhood Roots of Adult Happiness,* says that parents who provide too much for their children create "people who go through their adult lives chronically dissatisfied."[18] A culture of consumption creates a chronic state of discontent. Because we have few limits, we not only constantly want more, we also are less pleased with whatever we do have.

HOW WE GOT BRANDED

According to marketing and advertising expert James Twitchell, branding is a fairly recent development in human history. "Before the Industrial Revolution, soap was soap, malt liquor was malt liquor, the church was The Church." But the advent of factories, mass production and the rise of corporate identities meant that "soap became Ivory, malt liquor became Glenturret single-malt scotch whiskey, the church became Southern Methodist."[19] Industrial production arose at the same time as nineteenth-century Romanticism, which gave rise to "the startling contention that inanimate things and nonhuman life share feeling."[20] In other words, commodities could take on character traits. And indeed they did. They needed to. In order to distinguish between one kind of soap and another, companies told stories and narratives that imbued their products with particular personalities to be branded and marketed to their customers.

Companies have branded themselves and their products to be synonymous with particular traits: Nike = coolness. Disney = magic. Maytag = dependability. FedEx = overnight.[21] Consider how a Volkswagen Beetle feels more fun than a Volvo station wagon, or how iMacs and iPods successfully established themselves as markers of people who are cool and hip. Mountain Dew originally had a rural "hick" image, at one point using the tag line "Zero-proof hillbilly moonshine." By the 1990s Pepsi had successfully rebranded Mountain Dew to be identified with a particularly edgy kind of youth culture, using extreme sports imagery like inline skating on top of skyscrapers or off-road mountain biking to catch a cheetah that had stolen a can of Mountain Dew. It now sponsors ESPN's X-Games and other extreme sports to reinforce this brand image.[22]

Sociologically, when we as consumers purchase branded merchandise, we identify with a particular community. If we shop at the Warner Bros. store and buy clothing with the logos of certain television shows, we are saying that we want to be publicly identified as a fan of that show, and we want people to associate with us whatever positive (or negative) values and associations that show connotes. If we wear a Green Bay Packers sweatshirt or a Chicago Cubs ball cap, we are making known to the world that we derive some sense of identity in being part of that community that those sports teams call their fans.

We subconsciously identify with corporate icons and their personified spokesbeings. "The Marlboro Man invokes the independent outsider, Betty Crocker the archetypal good mother, and so forth."[23] The cigarette is merely an avenue to rugged individualism; the cake mix is the route to domestic goddessness. English pop artists Neil Cummings and Marysia Lewandowska say, "It is not objects that people really desire, but their lush coating of images and dreams. . . . [I]t is never the object which is consumed—instead, it is the relationship between us and the object of desire."[24] The meaning is not found in the actual product but the stories surrounding the product.

Whether the brand narratives are personified by actual people like Oprah Winfrey, Martha Stewart, Colonel Sanders, or Ben and Jerry, or fictional ones like Ronald McDonald or Aunt Jemima, or even nonhumans like the Pillsbury Doughboy, the Jolly Green Giant, the Energizer

Bunny or Tony the Tiger, each of these iconic figures embodies some sort of positive trait that is meant to be transferred from product to consumer via the brand identity.

Branding is really about "storifying things." Branding "is not so much the result of production as it is the result of consumption. It's the stories we're after as well as the material goods."[25] It's no accident that Disney describes its theme parks as the happiest places on earth. That's the story they want their visitors to enter into. Disney isn't just selling rides and stage shows; it's marketing a Magic Kingdom, a this-worldly alternative to the kingdom of God. The Romanticist impulse redirected spiritual yearnings and reattached them to earthly commodities and products. So instead of yearning for God or heaven, instead of entering into the Christian story, we lay claim to the stories of corporate advertisers.

So when we buy branded material, we should ask ourselves, *What does this product say that I'm saying about who I am? What story or narrative am I participating in? What am I (consciously or unconsciously) saying about what I value or what is important to me?* As an exercise, look around your home, on your shelves and in your closets. Pull out some items that are clearly a brand extension of some sort. Ask your friends or family members to evaluate them with you. Why do I have this item? What is it about the brand or identity that I find attractive? And is this healthy or unhealthy from a Christian perspective? If I have an entire house furnished with Coca-Cola paraphernalia, does that approach idolatry?

Put bluntly, it is a lie that any product is inherently better than another simply because of a logo on it. Twitchell says, "To curb our acquisitiveness we would have to de-brand: 'It's a scarf; it's not an Hermes scarf. It's a car; it's not a Lexus. You put it around your neck or on your feet or you drive it. It's carrying more freight than it really needs to.'"[26]

It's no mistake that most generic products are cheaper than name brands. After all, when we buy a branded product, we're not only paying for the product. We're also paying part of the cost of massive advertising budgets needed to create and maintain brand identity. Naturally, it's next to impossible to free ourselves completely from brand domination; even staples like toothpaste and toilet paper are carefully managed brand properties. But we can be alert to our tendencies to gravitate toward particular products simply because of ingrained patterns.

In high school I used a particular brand of hair gel, partially because the brand had some "coolness" connotation that was important to me as a teenager.[27] Even though I've long given up any illusion of being cool, I continued to use this particular brand for years out of habit. This brand of gel was pricier than others, and it started to get more expensive. I then discovered that I could get a different brand of gel in larger containers for almost half the cost. I tried this cheaper brand for a while, and it basically worked just as well as the more expensive stuff. So I switched brands. The associated value of the more prestigious brand identity was not worth it to me to pay an extra buck or two, especially when I no longer care what people think of my hair.

We all have our preferences; some things are more important to us than others. Some of us may be fiercely loyal to a particular breakfast cereal, and no generic substitutes will do. But we may be fine with whatever kinds of napkins or paper towels happen to be on sale this week. Others of us will insist on specialty shampoo, but it doesn't matter if our shoes are brand name or not. Some of us are picky about our coffee; maybe we are devoted to a particular toothpaste. That's all well and fine. But when we find ourselves reaching for a bag of chips simply because it has the latest movie tie-in advertised on it, that's when we need to have our internal radar bleep at us: "Don't be manipulated by this company's marketing department! Do you really need this?"

I have to admit, I am a sucker for new products. My personality type always wants to try whatever is new. My wife is the opposite. She is more prone to stick with the tried-and-true than to take a risk on an unknown quantity. Both of us need to be aware of our default tendencies. Ellen occasionally needs to reevaluate her shopping choices to consider whether it would be wiser or better to use a different product than the one she usually gets. And I need to make sure that I don't just buy the new flavor of ice cream or breakfast cereal because some product development department decided to throw some new flavors or colors into the mix. (I admit that I bought a box of red-and-blue "Spider-Berry" Spider-Man Pop-Tarts when *Spider-Man 2* was released. But I only got it when the grocery store was trying to get rid of it and selling it at half price.)

From a Christian perspective, the Christian story of creation, Fall, redemption and re-creation trumps all other stories. Indeed, most early advertising themes and motifs borrowed Christian narrative structure. You have a problem, like heartburn? You have a savior, an antacid. Many commercials use this salvific plotline. But Starbucks, Microsoft or Nike can't deliver us from evil or even inefficiency, untidiness or discomfort. As Christians, our hope is in Christ, not any corporate brand identity.

Of course, Christians are just as susceptible to Christian branding. It's not just that churches themselves have distinct brand identities as Vineyard rather than Episcopalian or emergent rather than fundamentalist. It's also that many churches are eager to adopt curricula or programming that has a certain seal of approval on it from a prominent megachurch or parachurch organization. Christian publishers now see their marquee authors as brand entities; big-name authors are not just people or personalities—they're brands, complete with brand managers who leverage the brands with ancillary products and extensions.

We need to repudiate the power of brands in defining our identities and determining our consumption. Christian consumerism or Christian consumption needs to be redemptive. It is to de-story the corporate brand connotations and to weigh them in light of the Christian story. In the Christian story shoes are functional footwear, not status symbols. Soap is just soap.

HOW IDENTITY SHAPES CONSUMPTION AND VICE VERSA

We have any number of conscious and unconscious filters that determine how we prioritize what we buy and where we shop. Our self-identity drives these decisions in ways that we may not even understand. For example, when you browse a mall, consider why you stop in some stores and not others. If you go into a shop that has trendy teen clothing, you are probably a teen with aspirations of being trendy. Some clothing stores are distinctively more upscale or downscale than others; some communicate an outdoorsy identity, others a sporty/athletic one, others a professional/corporate look. Your self-identity as one kind of person or another determines what kind of items you will shop for.

Identity shapes consumption. We tend to consume in ways that reflect our self-understanding of who we are. Much of my family's discretionary spending is driven by such identities as being parents and readers. As parents, we purchase educational videos for our kids. As readers, we buy Sue Grafton mysteries. But we aren't pet owners or particularly athletic. So we don't buy cat toys or sports equipment. Our identity determines that we will more frequently shop at Borders or Toys "R" Us than Sportmart or Petco. My wife's purchases of paper stock, stamps, ink pads and other such supplies only make sense if stamping fits in with her self-identity. If she didn't see herself as a stamper, or if stamping were contrary to her notion of self-understanding, then it would not be likely that she would purchase stamping supplies.

I mentioned this to my colleague Elaina, and she said, "That's why I return gifts that don't fit who I am. They're giving me an identity that I don't want." We tend to bolster our own identities by purchasing and consuming items that reinforce our sense of who we are or who we want to be.

If we self-identify as a vegetarian or a vegan, that directly determines the kinds of food we will buy and what aisles of the grocery store we will go down. A particular understanding of who we are will make us more likely to buy organic foods. The reasons behind purchasing organic foods may vary—we may do so out of conviction that they are healthier for us, or we may do so out of concern for how animals are treated, or we may connect such foods with Christian principles of stewardship and justice. No matter the reason or motive, we are more likely to purchase such foods if we have a self-identity of being the kind of person that buys and eats such foods.

If you want to understand someone's sense of self-identity, take a look at their coffee table and see what magazines they subscribe to. The magazines we read are a diagnostic indicator of how we perceive ourselves, what communities we belong to and what interests we value. Someone who reads *The Economist* and *BusinessWeek* probably has a very different sense of self than someone who reads *Road & Track, Martha Stewart Living, Field & Stream* or *Psychology Today*.

Look inside the magazines and examine the advertising. Here we see how consumption flows out of self-identity. A reader of *Saveur* magazine is far more likely to buy specialty wines or luxury refrigerators than someone who reads *Electronic Gaming Monthly. Sierra* has ads for hybrid cars and environmentally safe products. Some Christian magazines have ads for Christian cruises and jewelry. Browsing the magazine rack at a bookstore gives glimpses into the multiple subcultures, communities and identities people may have: *Wine Enthusiast, Cigar Aficionado, Yoga International, Working Mother, Golf Illustrated, Cookbook Digest.*

Consumption shapes identity. If identity shapes consumption, the reverse is also true. The more magazines we subscribe to, the more we will understand ourselves as members of those subcultures. The more stamping supplies my wife buys, the more likely she will see herself as a stamper. The more comic books I purchase, the more I understand myself as a collector of comic books. The more Blue's Clues videos my son watches, the more Blue's Clues shapes his thinking, vocabulary and categories for understanding the world and himself. The more we consume in particular patterns, the more we understand ourselves as that kind of consumer.

Community shapes identity. My colleague Dave and I once went to a gathering of Christians where many lived in intentional communities that raised their own food and were committed to organic or vegetarian lifestyles. For Dave and me, this was a new thing. But seeing intentional Christian communities live out shared meal preparation as an expression of Christian discipleship was quite compelling. The communal experience of eating organic meals together was more persuasive than reading a magazine article or brochure about the benefits of organic food. We heard stories from these communities about how significant their witness was as it related particularly to shared meal-making. Their practice is distinctly countercultural, given our privatized, individualistic fast-food culture.

One of the most compelling aspects of their community witness is the fact that they prepare and eat their meals together, a deeply biblical practice that is worth recovering. The sense of being a community that eats together in this distinctive way shapes their identity and in turn shapes their consumer choices. Someone living in such a community is more likely to pay more for organic foods because it is a practice that fits in and reinforces their sense of identity and is consistent with their community. In many ways community is prior to identity, and our consumption flows out of both our community and our identity.

My wife and I have stopped shopping at Wal-Mart for a number of reasons. We found their stores aesthetically unappealing, and we have read disturbing reports about their business and labor practices.[28] But we have made two main purchases from Wal-Mart: a number of bookshelves, and a toddler-sized set of Baby Snoopy table and chairs.

In both cases our prior identity and community preferences trumped our concerns about Wal-Mart's business ethics. We are book lovers working in the publishing industry, and the pragmatic need for inexpensive bookshelves outweighed our disdain for Wal-Mart. We are also fans of Snoopy and the Peanuts gang, and the Baby Snoopy table set matched a Baby Snoopy comforter and sheet set that we had gotten for our son

Josiah. So our unconscious self-identification as "people who like Snoopy" trumped our social concern, simply because Wal-Mart was the only place we had ever seen this particular Baby Snoopy table set for sale. Of course, such consumption cultivates further consumption; having Snoopy stuff makes us more likely to buy more Snoopy stuff to match. This is why many stores have chain exclusives where a particular kind of product line is only available there, to create return shoppers.

CONSUMING MORE CHRISTIANLY

In modern society, consumption is inescapable. So our question is not whether or not we consume, but in what ways and to what degree. In many ways it is easier to see how our identity drives our consumption when we are talking about lifestyles like vegetarianism or hobbies like surfing or golf. It is more difficult to see how Christian identity shapes our consumption. If our primary identity is as Christians and all other commitments are secondary, then how does being a Christian drive how we shop and consume?

It's not just that we purchase only explicitly Christian items, even if this were possible. While there is certainly a place for buying Christian videos and greeting cards, mere Christian commodification is not enough. After all, plenty of Jesus junk and Christian kitsch may be well-intentioned, but purchasing them is not necessarily an act of Christian discipleship. It's often just a Christian form of consumerism. Rather, how might we infuse all of our consumer choices with Christian perspective? Can we consume more Christianly?

Here's a simple case study—coffee. How does Christian identity shape how we consume coffee? First of all, on a most basic level, we decide whether to drink coffee at all. After all, caffeine is an addictive substance. Some of us have come to be overly dependent on coffee to get us going in the morning. The concept of the coffee break was originally developed by corporate and industrial managers trying to get more productivity and work out of tired workers. So coffee could be considered a tool of exploitation to be avoided.

If we decide to consume coffee, then we must ask how to do so most Christianly. Is it good stewardship to buy specialty coffees at two, three or four dollars a drink? Can we cut down our expenses by buying more basic versions of coffee or by decreasing our frequency of coffee drinking?

Furthermore, can coffee be purchased in such ways that support Christian concepts of mission and social justice? Christian coffee drinkers should be aware of socially responsible fair trade coffees that are grown and purchased in ways that are beneficial to local growers without exploitation. Christians concerned for environmental stewardship can also advocate and support coffee suppliers that do not destroy indigenous environments. My wife and I seek out organic fair trade, shade grown coffee in whole bean decaf if possible. It's complicated, but we invest more energy and money in these kinds of coffee because we have been persuaded of the economic and environmental virtue in doing so.

We can also buy coffee from companies that specifically benefit Christian growers and ministries. When our company changed coffee vendors, I encouraged the decision makers to get our coffee from a company founded by Christians that provides fair trade coffee. It makes sense for our Christian workplace to purchase its coffee strategically in ways that help global Christian mission.[29] Author Tom Sine observes:

> Our evangelical friends in these countries [Britain, Australia, New Zealand and Canada] typically have a much greater concern for the biblical call to work for justice, peace, reconciliation, and creation care than their counterparts in America. Most of the evangelical churches we work with in Britain sell "fair-trade" products such as tea and coffee in their foyers because they have a much higher level of global awareness about the workers being fairly compensated for their labor. We have yet to see fair-trade products promoted in American evangelical churches.[30]

I'm not saying that there's necessarily a distinctively Christian way of buying carrots or apples or that we need to purchase Christian socks and underwear. But there are certainly ways that our consumption might be more redemptive. Besides practicing frugality, simplicity and steward-ship, we can also support businesses and companies that treat their employees fairly and justly.

All of this begins with self-understanding and self-awareness. What sense of self-identity or community is shaping how you consume? How are your consumer choices shaping your identity? What magazines are on your coffee table, and what purchases have you made because of them? What brand stories or images have you bought into? On the other hand, has a particular Christian conviction led you to change any of your patterns of consumption? Has your church or Christian community helped you be more accountable in your consumer choices? How might your church wield its collective consuming power more Christianly?

Again, there are no easy answers to how we decide how to make our consumer decisions. Different Christians will be called to support different causes and industries because all of us have individual personalities, preferences and interests. But we can begin by detaching ourselves from the tyranny of corporate branding, repudiating the power of status markers, and understanding how our identity and community shapes our consumption. It is an act of spiritual formation for us to allow ourselves to be shaped by Christian values and virtues rather than consumerist ones. Then we will be more alert to how God may be leading us to exercise our consumption in ways more beneficial for the sake of the kingdom.

Won't You Be My Neighbor?

Moving from Anonymity to Community

*The idea of a modest dwelling all our own, isolated from the
problems of other people, has been our reigning metaphor of the good
life for a long time. It must now be seen for what it really is: an
antisocial view of human existence.*

James Howard Kunstler, *Home from Nowhere*

Charles Manelli grew up before World War II in an urban St. Louis
neighborhood. He describes his childhood environment this way:

> You had a parochial school on one corner, and down the street was
> the public school. It was a neighborhood, and it was like that all
> over the city. And everybody knew everybody, whether you went
> to parochial or public school, it was just a big neighborhood; you
> could walk anyplace in the whole area and you knew everybody.
> . . . We just played. We made up our own games. We played ball
> in the alleys and the vacant lots. We didn't need any supervision.

Eventually Manelli left the neighborhood and moved to the new postwar suburbs. "People our age at that time all wanted to buy houses, and
there just weren't any houses available in the city of St. Louis. So they all
moved, and bought homes out in the county. . . . The new subdivisions

were where the young people wanted to go."[1]

As a result, Manelli's children and grandchildren grew up in a very different world. His kids took the bus to school because it was too far to walk. Sports have also changed. "Everything's organized now. And you've got to drive to it. And you've got to wear uniforms." His wife, Anne, adds that they now live across the street from a park with a ballpark and soccer field. "You'll never see any one person just playing by themselves. When they're there, they're with an organized team, with coaches and the whole thing. . . . To just go over there, a bunch of kids getting together to just hit the ball around, or kick a soccer ball around, no. They don't do that."[2] Suburban culture has shifted youth from unsupervised, informal neighborhood play to organized, supervised league activities.[3]

Anne says, "There's no place around here to walk to. Not even a grocery store." After Anne developed cataracts, she could no longer drive. "So I was stuck here in this house, waiting for Chuck to take me any place and every place I wanted to go. That I was not prepared for." She eventually had operations on her eyes to restore her sight so she could drive again—a virtual necessity for suburban living. The bottom line: "In this neighborhood . . . we've been here thirty-five years now and we hardly know anybody."[4]

One of the biggest critiques of modern suburbia is the problem of suburban isolationism. While we may have a façade of community and neighborhood, we actually have clusters of autonomous individuals and atomized family units with no historic or natural connections to their neighbors.

When we speak of "community," we usually mean it in the sense of affinity groups, like the arts community, the African American community, the gay/lesbian community, the Christian community. Lost today is the sense of *physical* community, in which "community" refers to a particular geographic area or neighborhood that anchors us and defines us. "Community was once not something you chose; it was something you were a part of, that you only separated from with great effort and difficulty," observes commentator Alex Marshall. "The biggest change in 'community' is that it is less linked to a physical place than ever before."[5]

The average American moves every six years. The suburbs tend to be transient places where neighbors move in and out with little warning, and people don't stay long enough to feel a sense of attachment or investment in the local community. Thus it's less and less likely that we'll know our neighbors or even invest the energy to get acquainted.

"One of the biggest mistakes people make today is looking only to buy a house, not to find a neighborhood."

RANDY FRAZEE, *THE CONNECTING CHURCH*

At the end of the twentieth century futurist Faith Popcorn identified "cocooning" as one of the most significant trends of the contemporary era. "Cocooning is about insulation and avoidance, peace and protection, coziness and control—a sort of hyper-nesting."[6] This stay-at-home syndrome, as she characterized it, was heralded by the skyrocketing of VCRs, the use of answering machines to screen our calls and shopping at home. In the days before the Internet, Popcorn saw mail-order catalogs as a sign of the future of cocooning. Now we can do virtually all our shopping virtually—online. We can bank online, buy groceries online, custom order jeans online, date online, even have virtual doctor's appointments online. One person legally changed his name to Dot-ComGuy and spent an entire year in his home, doing everything online. He never had to leave the house.

Cocooning means that people get out less and stay home more. Commuter culture limits our time at home, so we isolate ourselves with our nuclear families and have little time for outside service or ministry. I once heard a pastor say that community has been replaced by cocoonity. How did we get here, and can we do anything about it?

THE UNINTENDED CONSEQUENCES OF AIR CONDITIONING AND TELEVISION

Suburbia was created at the same time that air conditioning became widely available. While summer heat once drove people to sit outside on their front porches, by the mid-twentieth century, people were able to stay indoors and relax in cool, air-conditioned comfort. Front porches used to be an architectural necessity. With the advent of central air, porch space could be fully enclosed and made into an additional room or parlor. Homes gradually shifted from having porches in front to having patios or decks out back. This diminished the opportunity for neighbors to see and interact with one another.

At the same time, media communication was making a quantum shift from the age of radio to the era of television. Radios were portable, and people could listen to a baseball game while sitting with friends on a front porch or working on a car in the garage. Not so with television. Instead of a radio traveling with you around the house, the television stayed put and drew family members to sit in front of it. So not only did air conditioning bring people indoors from their front porches but then television kept people inside and away from their neighbors. The end result was increased isolationism. While people were watching the same television shows on the three broadcast networks, they were doing so privately and noncommunally.

Air conditioning brought people indoors.
Television kept them there.

Television's power cannot be understated. In North America, "television viewing time is greater than that of all other forms of entertainment combined."[7] Most people watch an average of three or four hours of television a day—hours not spent in community or civic settings, connecting with neighbors or relating to others. While friends may occasionally watch particular TV shows together, the vast majority of television is watched in isolation from others. In fact, time spent watching TV eclipses the time that family members spend interacting with one another; spouses spend a daily average of four minutes conversing with each other and parents only *thirty seconds* talking with their children.[8]

The forms and genres of television programming have been shaped by suburban perspectives. For example, the narrative structures of soap operas (fragmented, repetitive and endless) were designed for the domestic schedule of the suburban wife, "always busy, always distracted, but always available for both story and advertising."[9] And while television programming and advertising often holds up an urban vision of what is cool and hip, the primary intended audiences are usually suburban viewers, the largest and most significant demographic in terms of disposable income.

In addition, the content of television programming has generally reinforced suburban ideals and concerns, with narrative themes principally "grounded in suburban, bourgeois experience."[10] Many television shows have been set in suburbia, from *Leave It to Beaver* and *The Brady Bunch* to *The OC* and *Desperate Housewives*. Even genres like westerns or sci-fi are crafted in such a way that the plots and themes are relevant to a modern suburban audience. Think of the family dramas of *Little House on the Prairie* or *Dr. Quinn, Medicine Woman*. While the structure of the shows were clothed in nineteenth-century frontier life, the lessons of family togetherness and community spirit learned in each episode were intended to be applied to the lives of suburban viewers—even if those viewers spent more time watching TV than actually interacting with each other or their neighbors.

SUBURBAN GEOGRAPHY AND SOCIOLOGY

My hometown of Bloomington, Minnesota, is an example of old and new suburbia coexisting in the same city. The eastern side of Bloomington, where I spent my elementary school years, is pre-World War II suburbia, laid out on a grid with all the streets at right angles and named and numbered in orderly, alphabetical sequence. This model of land development is found in both urban and rural settings, as small towns often patterned themselves after the densely designed neighborhoods of the big cities.

On the other hand, the western side of Bloomington, where I lived through junior high and high school, is postwar suburbia, characterized by streets that curve and loop, with circles and cul-de-sacs running a variety of ways through town. This street design was no accident. Curvy streets meant that cars must drive more slowly through a neighborhood. Circles and cul-de-sacs were even quieter because there was no through traffic. This made suburban neighborhoods safer for children to play in and less prone to noisy motorists. I lived in a circle, which meant that all the neighborhood kids could play in the street without having to worry about passing traffic. In the summer we'd play kick the can with the can in the middle of the circle. In the winter, the extra snow from the circle would be plowed into six-foot-high piles on our lawns, making for terrific snow forts. Occasionally, freezing rain would transform the circle into an informal ice rink, and we could actually ice skate on the street.

Suburban street layout can either foster community or prevent it, depending on what the designers intend. Some subdivisions are built so neighbors have a clear sense of "block" identity, and it's easy for residents to know who their neighbors are. Houses face each other, mailboxes might be adjacent, and human interaction is facilitated. On the other hand, some subdivisions seem to be designed for privacy. Houses may be quite far away and may not even be in view of each other on a curved street. Trees and shrubbery may be planted as barriers, or fences may separate neighbors from interaction. Some subdivisions lack sidewalks as well, preventing neighborhood walks and Halloween trick-or-treating.

Depending on your geography it may be relatively easy or downright difficult to interact with your neighbors. As socioeconomic class elevates, the privacy factor becomes more important. Bigger houses on larger lots mean that neighbors are spaced farther away from each other. Those who live near or in such houses must beware of the temptation to hide from neighbors or to assume that others would prefer not to have anything to do with you.

---

*"They want everything new but also a sense of place.
They also want community."*

DAVID BROOKS, *ON PARADISE DRIVE,* ON EXURBAN RESIDENTS

Despite suburban tendencies toward isolationism, people still yearn for community. The search for the suburban promised land is not limited to housing; suburbanites long for human connections as well. Case in point: When exurban growth exploded in the 1990s, many new home buyers wanted to live near golf courses; they wanted recreation. But by the year 2000, according to surveys done for the building industry, "prospective home buyers were less likely to demand country clubs in their new neighborhoods. Instead, they wanted walking paths, coffee shops, Kinko's, clubhouses, parks, and natural undeveloped land. In other words, they wanted community."[11] As a result, some new exurban housing developments are reinstituting a peculiar, antiquated architectural component: the front porch.

YEARNING FOR COMMUNITY

A number of forces have acted together toward the decline of community in modern life. Technological isolation, privatization of entertainment via the television and the computer, commuter culture via the automobile, increasing hecticness and busyness, and lack of public space and civic organizations all contribute. Both changes in human behavior as well as structural changes in suburban geography are at fault.

Studies have shown that suburbs have demonstrably less neighboring and community involvement than small towns. "Suburbs also are more private and anonymous, possibly because they are not 'whole' communities but only the residential piece. They lack the overlapping social networks found in small towns where people work and shop as well as live together."[12] Suburbs have more freedom, anonymity, delinquency and crime than small towns.

Oddly enough, studies of mid-twentieth-century suburbia found that suburbanites were *more* likely than those in urban environments to engage in social interaction with their neighbors, partly because of social homogenization. The demographics of suburbia meant that there were more families with young children who were likely to interact with one another.[13] However, demographic shifts are such that "married couples with children are no longer dominant in suburbs. They are outnumbered by young singles and the elderly living alone."[14] Increasing demographic diversity might mean that suburban residents have fewer natural reasons to connect with one another. No longer can it be assumed that each home includes a stay-at-home mom who brings her kids to the park to play with other moms and kids.

Furthermore, focus on the nuclear family diminishes community connections. According to the University of Michigan's Institute for Social Research, children today actually spend *more* time with their parents than they did in 1980.[15] (Much of this "time together" is spent watching television or movies, not interacting conversationally or recreationally.) But parents are not working less. Rather, the time that adults are carving out for family has been taken away from housework, leisure activities and adult friendships. In other words, parents are spending more time with their kids, but at the expense of larger community and church involvement.

While it is laudable for Christians to care for our own families, we need to beware of the temptation to overprioritize our children and nuclear families. If we turn inward and only focus on our children's activities, development and achievement, we inadvertently fall into idolatry.[16] Jesus would encourage us to be open toward the outsider and the community, not retreat into navel-gazing and cocoonity. In contrast, families together can enter into community service and ministry, and parents can serve others alongside their children rather than spend the majority of their time on their own private development and accomplishments.[17]

Not only are we getting out less, we are also having people over less. According to Robert Putnam, "In 1975 the average American entertained friends at home 15 times per year; the equivalent figure is now barely half that."[18] In other words, most people now host friends over less than once a month. This statistic seemed unusually low to me, but then I flipped through our family's guest book. Some calendar years, we had record of hosting guests for dinners or parties only eight or nine times a year.

Consider also the phenomenon of the "playdate." No longer do parents spontaneously drop in on their neighbors for a cup of coffee while the kids play in the backyard. Now parents need to schedule playdates much as they would schedule any other appointment. Both families must find an opening in their daily planners, often a narrow window between other scheduled activities rather than an open-ended time. And it is less likely that such playdates will happen locally within a neighborhood. Like everything else in modern suburban life, a playdate requires a commute.

If our community participation has been declining, what, if anything, is replacing it? James Twitchell proposes that the decline of social capital parallels the rise of brand identities and affiliations. As society becomes more commercial and consumerist, our sense of self-identity is less and less in any physical gatherings of people and more and more in the imagined and virtual communities of consumer demographics. In short, our communities are no longer with the Kiwanis or the PTA but rather in nonphysical communities of people who watch a particular television show or drink a particular kind of soft drink. "Hard to believe," says

Twitchell, "but knowing what's in a Big Mac (two all-beef patties, a special sauce . . .) has much of the same kind of unifying force as knowing who played third base for the Yankees, which, in a way, has the same force as knowing what's in Deuteronomy 2:18."[19]

While shared socializing is declining, shared pop cultural understanding and brand consumption and participation are increasing. Far more people wear Nike or Tommy Hilfiger branded clothing than sweatshirts from the local high school marching band booster club. Brand knowledge of commercial jingles and corporate logos transcends local geography, socioeconomic status, race, ethnicity or religious background. As consumers we imagine ourselves as members of particular communities, even if those communities never gather in any physical, embodied way. I am a "valued member of the eBay community," though I never meet anyone I buy from or sell to.

In today's consumer culture branded identity and affiliation may actually lead to some alternative version of community. I have read articles about eBay conventions where eBay buyers and sellers gather to celebrate their common interests and help one another further their business. Some people have met via eBay and gotten married at these conventions. Whereas previous generations met their sweethearts and spouses in high school and the junior prom, today marital unions can come about as an inadvertent result of online commerce. And when couples marry at Disney World or in the sports arena of their favorite professional ball team, it says something about the brand communities that have supplanted what used to be the cornerstone of community and family, in those quaint old days where people met and married in the churches that they worshiped in.

STARBUCKS, "THIRD PLACES" AND COMMUNITY

A few years ago I read the corporate biography of Starbucks, written by Howard Schultz, Starbucks's chairman and CEO. He tells the story of how Starbucks grew from just one store in Seattle to the world's biggest coffee chain. When Starbucks started out, they only sold coffee beans, coffee grinders, and other coffee equipment and paraphernalia. They didn't brew any coffee in their stores. They didn't serve actual coffee.

Then in 1983, Schultz went on a business trip to Italy. There he noticed an espresso bar by his hotel. The aroma drew him in, and he got a cappuccino. Then he noticed that there were two other espresso bars down the block, and more on every street. Each one was unique, with a slightly different personality. They were all filled with people, talking, chatting and drinking coffee. Here's how Schultz describes it:

> The energy pulses all around you. Italian opera is playing. You can hear the interplay of people meeting for the first time, as well as people greeting friends they see every day at the bar. These places, I saw, offered comfort, community, and a sense of extended family.[20]

That's when Schultz had his aha moment. He realized that even though he was in the coffee business, he was doing it all wrong. He had seen coffee merely as a product, a commodity to be sold, not something with the potential to build relationships and community. So Schultz came back to the U.S. and started changing Starbucks. He began brewing coffee in his stores. He set up chairs and started playing music. And Starbucks was transformed, from just being another retail outlet into a place where coffee became an experience, where people could meet and talk and linger, where people built relationships and community.

Starbucks had exponential growth during the 1990s. Schultz writes, "In the 1990s, coffee bars became a central component of the American social scene in part because they fulfilled the need for a nonthreatening gathering spot, a 'third place' outside of work and home."[21] Schultz borrowed this idea of "third places" from sociologist Ray Oldenburg, who defines them in his book *The Great Good Place* as "public places that host the regular, voluntary, informal, and happily anticipated gatherings of individuals beyond the realms of home and work."[22] Many cultures around the world had these third places, such as beer gardens in Germany, pubs in England or cafés in France. "America once had such spots, in its taverns, barbershops, and beauty parlors. But with suburbanization, they are vanishing, replaced by the self-containment of suburban homes."[23]

One reason Starbucks in particular and coffeehouses in general have become so widespread is there aren't many places in our society where people can build community. Starbucks capitalized on this need for community and filled the vacuum. Schultz says that "Americans are so hungry for a community that some of our customers began gathering in our stores, making appointments with friends, holding meetings, striking up conversations with other regulars." Once Starbucks understood this sociological and psychological need for third places, they responded with larger stores with more seating as well as live music in some locations. Teens who grew up hanging out in shopping malls became twenty-somethings who hang out in cafés and coffeehouses, where "the music is quiet enough to allow conversation. The places are well-lit. No one is carded, and no one is drunk."[24]

Yet Starbucks's success only goes so far. While Starbucks may provide an inviting atmosphere and a context where people can connect, it's not truly a public meeting place for civic interaction. You might go there with your friends, but you don't necessarily go to Starbucks to meet strangers and engage neighbors. In the end, Starbucks is still a commercial enterprise, selling lattes and Frappuccinos. You might experience a little more sense of community in a Starbucks than you would picking up a coffee from a drive-through, but the $4.76 you pay for your drink is also paying for the comfy environment. Starbucks isn't only selling coffee; it's also selling the image (some would say illusion or façade) of community.

Schultz thinks that Starbucks actually meets that need for community. Coffeehouses do have a sociological function in that they provide a nonthreatening gathering place that acts as a needed alternative to work and home. But they are not neutral space. At best, Starbucks and the like are a half-measure. Many coffeehouses and other such institutions welcome community organizations, support groups and other gatherings in their stores, which serves the dual purpose of offering a place for groups to meet and also drawing more customers into their doors and selling more cappuccino. It is commercially advantageous to the proprietors to have community events in their stores. Likewise, bookstores have cafés because studies have found that a customer with a coffee is more likely to browse longer and purchase more.

Even so, this doesn't preclude the possibility of real connections and relationships taking place in such a commercial setting. On the one hand, it may be an exercise of hospitality to invite a friend over to your house for a visit. On the other hand, it may contribute to civic capital to meet at a nearby coffeehouse or public park instead. Getting out of the house on occasion may moderate our tendency toward suburban isolation and privacy. And being in a public or semipublic environment can allow for the opportunity to interact with people whom God might bring across our path.

I know several writers who do much of their writing at the local coffee shop or bagel place. They are such regulars there that they have come to know the baristas at the counter and some of the other denizens who stop in regularly.[25] Frequenting a local establishment regularly can build familiarity with both employees and customers, opening the possibility of actual connections and even evangelistic witness. Bill Hybels and Mark Mittelberg call this "strategic consumerism." If you shop at the same places over and over, you may well build relationships with the people you see there. They write,

> When we frequent their place of business with courtesy and concern for their welfare, it's pretty easy to get on a friendly first-name

basis. The relationship will grow as we show genuine interest in their life, their family, their work and their hobbies. Over time, we'll begin to earn their trust and pique their curiosity about what it is that makes us different from so many other customers who don't seem to care about them at all.[26]

Not that this is a license for conspicuous consumption, but we can shop in such a way that opens us to connecting with others. The cashiers will no longer seem as anonymous. I am such a regular at my local library that if I come in to pick up reserve books, they recognize me on sight and get my books for me even before they scan my library card. The proprietors of several local used-book stores know me by name.

While it may be intrusive to strike up a conversation with a total stranger, it may be less threatening to do so if you see the person regularly every morning for coffee. After nodding politely at each other for some time, you may well move to actual conversation. We need not assume that suburbia means that we are atomized individuals who never interact. We can suppress our impulses to ignore those around us and instead try to live in awareness and attentiveness to those we encounter, whether at a park or playground or in a restaurant or grocery store.

The need for a third place outside work and home ultimately points us toward something else—the church. We will explore the topic of the suburban church in chapter eight, but for now, it is enough to say that all of us are hard-wired for community and relationships. We and our suburban neighbors yearn for third places where we can make deep connections, and the suburban Christian is called to foster these relationships both individually and corporately.

THE COMMUNAL POWER OF TUPPERWARE

If such inventions as air conditioning and television tended to isolate us and fragment community, other things have some potential to counteract suburban isolationism and foster community. Case in point: Tupperware.

The first Tupperware product, a seven-ounce milky white polyethylene container, was manufactured by the Tupper Corporation in 1939. Tupperware initially struggled with selling in department stores and through mail order. Saleswoman Brownie Wise, the first woman to appear on the cover of *BusinessWeek,* demonstrated Tupperware products to groups of enthusiastic homemakers, and the Tupper Corporation adopted the "Party Plan" system in 1951. Soon Tupperware merchandise was distributed exclusively through the Tupperware party. "By 1954 over twenty thousand women belonged to the Tupperware party network as dealers, distributors and managers."[27]

Prior to the Tupperware party, products were mostly sold in distant department stores or door to door. The Tupperware party created a whole new experience by incorporating party games, refreshments, gifts and prizes into product demonstrations. It blended domesticity with commerce and transformed friends into customers. Tupperware dealers often encouraged social clubs and civic groups to host parties as fundraisers. As a result, suburban homemakers used their hospitality, management skills and social networks to generate additional income and foster community spirit. "Tupperware, a product which developed contemporaneously with postwar suburbia, wholeheartedly embraced domesticity and conspicuous consumption," writes historian Alison Clarke. "The Tupperware Party became an emblem of suburban life."[28]

Tupperware dealers were given various incentives and rewards for their success, including vacations, washing machines and convertibles. But the social and community benefits were perhaps the more significant motivational factors. "Women were unified in their desire not just for material luxuries, but for a sense of belonging. Becoming a dealer or manager meant having a large network of social relations, extra money and a standing in the community."[29] One woman said, "Before I attended a Tupperware Party I thought the last thing I'd like to do was sit with a whole load of other homemakers and talk recipes. But I had a sociable time and it helped me with my first boy, 'cos you know I wasn't so confident about child care in them days."[30]

Modern-day inheritors of the Tupperware model include such companies and industries as Creative Memories scrapbooking, PartyLite candles and Pampered Chef cooking utensils. My wife is hosting a Stampin' Up party as I write this. She and some friends are joyously working with card stock, rubber stamps and colored ink pads to create their own greeting cards and other personalized paper products. I hear a lot of laughter and fun being had, even as products are demonstrated and items are purchased. The presenter is training the attendees to become stampers, and as their identity as stampers is forged, so too is increased the likelihood that they will become purchasers of stamping supplies. One of the relational dynamics of such parties is that there is a more-than-subtle pressure for people to buy items, if only out of friendship to the host. It is a rare person who departs such a party without having bought an item.[31]

When Tupperware parties began, they primarily served to change noncommercial relationships of friends, neighbors and relatives into commercial relationships. Today, however, many relationships with co-workers and colleagues are relatively impersonal and transactional. Ironically, a Pampered Chef or Creative Memories party can actually help develop such impersonal relationships into more genuine friendships.

Another irony is that in the early days of Tupperware, social networks were such that hostesses invited neighbors on their block. Today, in our fragmented commuter culture, those hosting parties are more likely to invite friends and colleagues from work and church who live nowhere near the host home. It is less likely that people will invite their actual geographic neighbors.

How should Christians view these product parties? Like most other aspects of suburban life, they are a mix of pro and con, and Christians would do well to exercise wise discernment in stewardship, seeing in them both the potential for building community but also the customary suburban temptation for consumption. A stamping party is a place where participants consume and purchase products but also exercise creativity and craft-making. In some ways, such gatherings echo the quilting bee, in which people gather both to collaborate on some creative activity but more significantly to foster relationships and friendships. A better alternative would be noncommercial gatherings where friends and neighbors spend time knitting or scrapbooking together, sharing ideas and building community without financial transactions or sales pitches.

PRACTICING HOSPITALITY, CREATING COMMUNITY

The chief antidote to suburban anonymity and isolationism may well be the Christian practice of hospitality. Hospitality can be a profoundly prophetic, countercultural activity that helps us escape our cocoons, connect with our neighbors and minister to our communities. "Hospitality is central to the meaning of the gospel," writes ethicist Christine Pohl. "Because hospitality is basic to who we are as followers of Jesus, every aspect of our lives can be touched by its practice."[32]

Despite all the challenges and pressures of suburban life, the route to recovering a deeper sense of community is as basic as "love your neighbor." The principle may seem simplistic, but living it out in our suburban context will necessarily be as complex, varied and unique as each of us. We can come to see every interaction with neighbors, merchants and strangers as an opportunity to extend hospitality and welcome others in the name of Christ. Here are a number of ideas, and I trust that you and your friends could generate dozens more ways that this could be lived out in your own lives.

Our friends Andy and Phyllis are famed for their practice of hospitality. They have chosen to regularly host people in their home, often for weeks or months at a time. Their four kids grew up thinking it perfectly normal to have nonrelatives living with them for extended periods. Sometimes they host international students for a semester or a year or more. Other times their guests include people relocating, temporarily displaced by housing renovation, job transition or family crisis. Now with an empty nest with plenty of open bedrooms, rather than downsizing to a smaller home or converting the bedrooms into offices or dens, Andy and Phyllis continue to welcome the alien and stranger and demonstrate Christian love and hospitality.

Most of us invite people over to our homes less than eight times a year. Why not set a goal of having guests over at least once a month? Find ways to have friends or neighbors over for dinner, parties or backyard cookouts. Develop new traditions, annual holiday get-togethers or other such celebrations as ways to build hospitality as a rhythm of your life.

When Ellen and I were first married, we lived in an apartment complex. We didn't get to know very many of our neighbors, and we figured that would happen more naturally if we lived in our own home. After we moved to a townhouse, we found that we still didn't get to know many neighbors. We figured we'd get to know more people once we had kids and our kids played with neighbor kids. Then we had kids, and we got to know a few more neighbors through our kids. But not many more. The lesson, perhaps, is that there is no time like the present! If we keep on waiting for new situations or more optimal scenarios to make connections, we will find ways to keep waiting indefinitely. Seize the day and make the most of the opportunities before you.

My colleague Jeff has a neighbor down his block who acts as a catalyst in helping neighbors get to know one another. She goes to neighbors to borrow mayonnaise or Crisco, and invites others to borrow such staples from her anytime. She hosts Oscar parties for the neighborhood. When Jeff, who doesn't have cable TV, wanted to watch a broadcast on a cable news channel, he went over to this neighbor's house to watch the segment. Jeff now knows most of his neighbors seven or eight houses down the block in either direction, and he credits this woman as helping that happen. A certain kind of personality and initiative can break through the inertia of suburban isolationism and create community for a whole neighborhood.

One transferable principle is that perhaps we should not be so quick to go to the grocery store when we run out of things. One of the traits of suburban culture is easy access to goods. If we run out of milk, we go to the convenience store to pick up a gallon. If we need light bulbs or sugar or duct tape, it's simple enough to run to the store and buy some. In other words, we provide for ourselves. We don't allow others to provide for us, nor do we provide for others. Is it too radical a suggestion to say that perhaps we shouldn't always buy everything we need? Are there times where the community might be better off if neighbors depended on one another every once in a while?

This also applies to larger things, like appliances. Many have observed that most suburban house owners really don't need their own lawn-mower. Why not share a lawnmower with two or three other neighbors? Chances are that you wouldn't all need it at the same time, and it would only require a minimum of planning to decide how it is used and stored. Besides avoiding duplication of purchases and saving some garage space, you also increase the amount of interaction and interdependence be-tween neighbors. Some neighborhoods draw up community asset lists so neighbors are aware of what resources are available for sharing.

Once while our toddler was potty-training, he made a deposit in our upstairs toilet that impeded normal flushing. It would have been easy enough to go to the store and buy a plunger for a couple of bucks. But then I recalled Richard Foster's admonition to not always go out and pro-vide for ourselves, to allow God and the Christian community to provide as well.[33] So I went to a neighbor in our subdivision and borrowed two plungers from them. It solved the problem in no time and restored bath-room happiness. While it was no big deal, it was a baby step away from self-reliance and toward community interaction and neighborliness. I felt a little goofy walking down the block carrying two toilet plungers, but I felt the satisfaction of having spoken to a neighbor face to face that day.

Garages are another distancing factor contributing to suburban isolation and alienation. In many neighborhoods, the garage door goes up,
the car goes in or out, and the garage door goes down. There's no chance
for human interpersonal contact or conversation. Perhaps we could
counter this suburban tendency toward privacy by occasionally parking
on our driveways or on the street, if permitted by local ordinances. Walk
a little farther to and from your house. Wash your car in your driveway.
Increase the possibility of interacting with neighbors. Don't be so quick
to retreat indoors.

Garages can even be transformed for alternate uses. I heard about one
man who converted his garage into a mini community center where
neighborhood children could gather and play. This created opportunities for ministry and outreach with children and parents alike.

I have always loved lemonade stands, both as a proprietor in my
childhood and as a customer in adulthood. These days many residential
blocks have very little pedestrian traffic, and often kids sit forlornly at
their roadside tables watching the cars speed by. So when I can, I stop at
these stands and buy a Dixie cup of lukewarm red Kool-Aid for a quarter.
Not only is it gratifying to see the kid's face light up, I am both encouraging youthful entrepreneurship and making a human connection in a
local neighborhood. My wife thinks I go overboard when I deliberately
look for lemonade stands (she thinks they should be cited for health
code violations), but I see it as an opportunity to be neighborly.

---

*"One of the simplest and most practical things you can do to create
community in your neighborhood is to play in the front yard."*

RANDY FRAZEE, *THE CONNECTING CHURCH*

We can also run our daily errands in ways that contribute to community and relationships. I remember reading an article exhorting fathers

to bring their sons with them whatever they happened to be doing. Our older son, Josiah, enjoys going grocery shopping and seeking out items like a treasure hunt. Need to pick up something? Bring your kids along. Have something to do at church? Invite a neighbor to join you. Let others participate in your life, even in the boring, ordinary details.

Some neighborhoods have even rehabbed their physical environments to be more conducive to community. Neighbors remove fences and create shared common areas where families can play and eat together. Many subdivisions already have common clubhouses or pool areas; these are opportunities to build community identity. Some have community newsletters and activities, progressive dinners and block parties and the like. The possibilities are endless.

Ultimately, we must come to view our suburbs not merely as private dwelling places but as communities where we know and are known by networks of neighbors and friends. No one is an island; extroverts and introverts alike need community. Even in suburbia. May the Lord open doors for us to practice hospitality and connect with our communities in ways that are genuine and life-giving and that help us all enter into the divine community of Father, Son and Holy Spirit.

FINDING GOD IN THE SUBURBS

Cultivating Spirituality in Everyday Life

When you live in a shopping mall where everything
bears a human imprint, who do you worship?

BILL MCKIBBEN, *THE COMFORTING WHIRLWIND*

Douglas Coupland's oft-quoted novel *Life After God* describes how Generation X grew up as the first generation raised without religion. What is not always noticed is that he is specifically describing the youth of a *suburban* setting.

> As suburban children we floated at night in swimming pools the temperature of blood; pools the color of Earth as seen from outer space. . . . Life was charmed but without politics or religion. It was the life of children of the children of the pioneers—life after God— a life of earthly salvation on the edge of heaven.[1]

Are people in suburbia less likely to have religious commitments? Is suburbia a threat to Christian spirituality?

One of the ironies of the suburban context is that even though some of the creation of suburbia is due to deeply spiritual hopes and longings, everyday life in suburbia seems to obliterate the need for God. The material realities of suburbia often blind us to invisible spiritual realities. As author Craig Gay puts it, the way of the modern world is that it's tempting to live as if God doesn't exist. Modern worldliness or secularism is usually not so much hostile to God, but "more commonly simply *indifferent* to the existence and reality of God."[2] Technological society makes God largely irrelevant, and modern institutions tend to operate with an assumption "that even if God exists he is largely irrelevant to the real business of life."[3]

Even faithful Christians are sucked into the temptation to live as if God doesn't exist, because in suburbia it is too easy to go about daily life without ever needing to think about God. We may be Christians, but we act like deists, as if God wound up the world like a clock and let it run. This is the temptation of "practical atheism." Even if we believe in God, our actions say that it doesn't really matter if God exists or not.

And yet there is hope for suburban spirituality. The suburbanite narrator of Coupland's novel, by the end of the book, comes to the realization that he does in fact need God after all. "My secret is that I need God," he writes. "I need God to help me give, because I no longer seem to be capable of giving; to help me be kind, as I no longer seem capable of kindness; to help me love, as I seem beyond being able to love."[4] The seeming absence of God actually points the character to his need for God. A generation of suburbanites that is living life after (post-) God can indeed be transformed into people that are living life after (in the pursuit of) God.[5]

In this chapter we'll explore some of the suburban forces that militate against awareness of God and what we can do to recover the practice of Christian spirituality in our suburban context. Suburbia leaves us and many of our neighbors spiritually empty, yearning for true significance and meaning. Suburbia affects us spiritually, but ancient spiritual disciplines and Christian perspectives can counter secularization and bring new vitality to our lives.

THE ABSENCE OF SCARCITY

I heard a news piece that described how a rural family needs to drive fifty miles to the nearest town to run their errands. They take a whole day each week to go into town, where they get supplies and groceries, have doctor and dentist appointments, and take care of business. They need to plan carefully, because storms or blizzards can trap them at their home without access to emergency care or adequate food or supplies.

This is not a situation that one typically sees in the suburbs. In suburbia we are never more than a few blocks away from a grocery store, convenience store or strip mall. Resources are readily available, often twenty-four hours a day. Thus those of us in the suburbs need not worry as much about having supplies on hand; if we run out of milk, it only takes a few minutes to pick up a gallon at the corner store.

This abundant availability subtly influences our perspective on life. We may come to believe the myth that such abundance is normative and universal. It makes us forget that many communities and nations around the world do not have such easy access to things we take for granted, like food and clean water. Our store shelves are rarely empty or unstocked, leading to the illusion that resources are unlimited. This can be a barrier to good stewardship. We are less likely to be frugal if we can always get more of whatever we want. We are less likely to worry about wasting fuel if we can fill up with gas anytime without worrying if the gas station pumps will run out.

Besides all the effects of commercial culture on our patterns of consumption, more significantly, we are less likely to depend on God for his provision when it is all too easy to provide for ourselves. We rarely pray for God to provide our next meal for us; more often we simply give cursory thanks for the food we already have.

But we need to recognize that the abundance that we see around us is illusory. Yes, grocery stores and shopping centers are stocked full of goods, but this blinds us to the fact that for a significant percentage of the population, affording even basic staples of life is a challenge. We forget that poverty hides in suburban settings. "We think of the suburbs as middle-class, but 46 percent of all people living under the poverty line reside in the suburbs."[6] Commercial abundance dulls our sensitivity to care for the poor because it creates the false impression that there can't be any poverty around us if all these goods are available. Dallas Willard suggests that one practice that can counteract this is for us to

> do grocery shopping, banking, and other business in the poorer areas of the city. This has an immense effect on our understanding of and behavior toward our neighbors—both rich and poor—and upon our understanding of what it means to love and care for our fellow human beings.[7]

Not only should Christians respond to consumer culture by exercising personal self-discipline, frugality and stewardship, we should also look outward beyond ourselves and seek out the disenfranchised whom God may be calling us to serve.

As an act of solidarity with those in the developing world who do not have enough to eat, biblical scholar John Stott does not take second helpings of food at meals.[8] This is a Christian practice of self-imposed scarcity to remind us that our resources aren't infinite and that God is our only true source of provision. We must refute the lie that we provide for ourselves. Recovering a sense of scarcity and dispelling the illusion of abundance heightens our sensitivity to those in need and propels us into Christian service to the poor and hungry. Then when we pray "Give us this day our daily bread," we may be God's avenue for answering that prayer for others.

THE ABSENCE OF HARDSHIP

Michele Rickett, founder and president of the mission organization Sisters In Service, and writer Kay Strom were meeting with a group of "untouchable" Dalit women in India. These women had never met a North American. They asked Kay, "Did you ever go hungry because you're a Christian?"

"No," Kay said. "I never did."

"Did you ever have your house taken away?" they asked. "Did you ever lose your job because you're a Christian? Has anyone ever thrown you in a fire because you are a Christian?"

"No," Kay responded uncomfortably. "In America those things don't happen."

The Dalit women stared uncomprehendingly. Then one said, "But if it doesn't cost you anything, how do you in America know what it means to be a Christian?"[9]

Christians in other parts of the world, especially those experiencing direct persecution or hardship, generally have a heightened sense of their need and dependence on God. Following Christ is tremendously costly. It can mean expulsion from one's home and community or imprisonment, torture, rape or death.

Not so in suburbia, where our spiritual awareness is often blunted by our general sense of safety and comfort. In a religiously pluralistic context where freedom of religion is the law of the land, Christians tend not to experience overt persecution and opposition. The threats to suburban Christians are far more subtle: materialism, secularism and the temptation to live as if God does not exist.

It's fine to believe in God in suburbia, but such religion is often little more than a private idiosyncrasy, a mere item of cognitive assent or a vague sense of spirituality. More subversively, secular pluralism may well be a greater threat to Christian faith than outright hostility against it. After all, when faith is repressed, it is often kindled and grows. But when God seems irrelevant to daily life, we lose sight of God. And more ominously, we begin to assume particular things about God or how life is supposed to be.

During another trip with Sisters In Service, Michele and Kay met a Chinese woman in Beijing who told them:

> You Americans think life is supposed to be pleasant. When it's not, you think something is wrong. You have to fix it so you can be happy and comfortable again. You have not learned to trust God when life is hard. You have not learned the lesson of finding his purposes for you when you are uncomfortable. You have not yet learned to find joy in suffering.[10]

We suburban Christians must resist the lie that comfort and painless existence are the ultimate ideals. Our goal is not a life without pain, though we may do what we can to alleviate others' suffering. Our call is to live a life of faithful witness even in the midst of difficulty, pain and suffering. Through hardship we grapple with ultimate issues, and our soul is formed in Christlikeness. As Aleksandr Solzhenitsyn wrote of his imprisonment in the Soviet gulag:

> It was only when I lay there on rotting prison straw that I sensed within myself the first stirrings of good. . . . I turn back to the years of my imprisonment and say, sometimes to the astonishment of those around me, "Bless you, prison!" . . . I nourished my soul there, and I say without hesitation: *"Bless you, prison*, for having been in my life!"[11]

Suburban comfort accustoms us to avoidance of uncomfortable situations at home, and some of us may be more comfortable going on a short-term mission trip overseas than talking to neighbors in our own hometowns. Doug Pagitt is the pastor of Solomon's Porch, an innovative emergent church in urban Minneapolis. I was in a discussion group where Pagitt told a story about going to a psychic fair nearby the church, where a person "read his aura." Someone in the group observed that most Christians would rather go on a mission trip to Africa before they would risk going to a psychic fair in their own neighborhood.

The Christian story is one of displacement and discomfort. For some of us God might upset our comfortable lives by sending us overseas to experience desperate poverty and persecution. For others God might call us to say hello to the Muslim family next door or the secular atheist at the grocery store. Either action, however large or small it may seem, however disruptive of our sense of comfort, may be God's path for our spiritual maturity.

We suburban Christians would do well to heed the lessons of the Old Testament. When the Israelites wandered in the wilderness, they longed for the foods of Egypt, despite the fact that they had been in slavery there. Once in the Promised Land, they fell into spiritual complacency, and during the time of the judges they all did what seemed right in their own eyes. During the era of the monarchy God sent his prophets to call Israel back to faithful living and concern for the poor and disenfranchised. Ultimately Jerusalem fell and Israel was sent into exile, where they rediscovered some sense of dependence and need for God.

We should beware of being lulled into spiritual complacency by living in suburban comfort. It may take upheaval and exile, either on a personal or societal level, to recalibrate our sensitivity and remind us to live in active dependence on God.

RELEARNING DEPENDENCE ON GOD

If our suburban lifestyles are too affluent and too comfortable for us to experience God's active presence and guidance, then we can take intentional steps to relearn how to be dependent on God for his provision. One basic way is to try to stop providing for ourselves and allow God the space to provide in ways other than our own means.

Richard Foster writes, "When you decide that it is right for you to purchase a particular item, see if God will not bring it to you without your having to buy it."[12] He tells a story of a friend of his who needed a pair of gloves for work. Rather than immediately go to the store to pur-

chase a pair, he instead prayed about it. A few days later, someone happened to give him a pair of gloves, even though he had not mentioned
his need for gloves to anyone! Foster says, "The point is not that he was
unable to buy the gloves; he could have done that quite easily. But he
wanted to learn how to pray in ways that might release money for other
purposes."[13]

I have had similar experiences on occasion. One winter I lost my
scarf, and I decided that scarves were inessential and that I would do
without rather than purchase another one. Then a friend from church
happened to mention to me, "Al, I've got an extra scarf. Would you like
it?" The timing of it indicated to me that I should receive this as a gra-
cious gift from God, that he was providing a little thing for me as an alternative to me providing it for myself. It was an opportunity to see how
the body of Christ ought to be providing for one another, sharing resources and giving and receiving freely. And it encouraged me to follow
my friend's example and be more generous to others.

This doesn't mean that we stop shopping entirely and expect God to
drop groceries on our front step. We ought to continue to exercise our
normal sense of responsibility in providing for the needs of our families
and others. Nor does it mean that we adopt a prosperity gospel approach
to the Christian life, like the college student who actually prayed, "Father, you know I need a new truck, so right now I just claim a Toyota
4x4, 3.4 liter, six-cylinder, extended cab . . . red with white trim. I need
low payments and affordable insurance."[14]

No, a healthy dependence on God will mean that we are in honest di-
alogue with God about our desires and allow him to help us discern if
they are wants or needs, necessities or luxuries. It is a mindfulness about
the Lord as our Shepherd, of Jesus as the good Shepherd and us as his
sheep, who must trust him for daily bread. We can meditate on Psalm
23 and rediscover, "I shall not want." We go through life wanting so
much, and yet—we shall not want! Sometimes the Shepherd will tell us

that we don't need something. Other times he will tell us that we're try-ing too hard to forage for food on our own, when he has our meals al-ready prepared for us. Sometimes he will delight us with surprise gifts, and our cup runneth over. All of this is to be experienced in dynamic re-lationship with the God who is truly present. If we consciously appre-hend his presence in our lives, we will go a long way toward dispelling the practical atheism that engulfs us.

LIVING IN AN UNNATURAL WORLD

Suburbia: Where they tear out trees
and then name streets after them.
BUMPER STICKER

One day while driving through a nearby suburb, I noticed that a street is named "Lakeview Terrace." There is no lake in view anywhere nearby. Nor is there any sign of a terrace. Writer and pastor Barbara Brown Tay-lor observes:

Where I live, subdivisions spring up in cow pastures like mush-rooms overnight. Since they all look the same, developers work hard to give them distinctive names. One is called "Harbor View," although the nearest body of water is thirty miles away. Another is called "Autumn Breeze," although that is only true for three months of the year. What the words mean is beside the point. It is what they seem to mean that counts. Their value lies in the fantasies they inspire.[15]

Suburbia is a place where humans are at the center of the universe. All the commercial entities, housing and traffic routes exist for human convenience, to allow us to live and work and eat and play. Not so in wil-derness areas. There we are shown that human beings are clearly not at the center of the universe. All you have to do to be reminded of this is to go hike without a compass in the woods where there is no trail. If you get lost, it's because nature did not bother to place any clearly marked signs for you. Nature is inconvenient for humans because it simply exists on its own terms.

Christian environmentalist and ethicist Bill McKibben makes an interesting observation about the book of Job. When Job complains to God, God's response is to describe the wonders of the natural world. God explains how things work, in ways that few humans would ever notice or understand. God is describing a world where people are not at the center. We are certainly part of creation, but we are not the center of it.

> God seems untroubled by the notion of a place where no man lives—in fact, God says he makes it rain there even though it has no human benefit at all. God makes the *wilderness blossom*—what stronger way could there be to make the point, what more overpowering fact to rebut the notion that we are forever at the center of all affairs.[16]

McKibben notes that most cultures have put God or nature or some combination thereof at the center of their lives. But we late-modern Westerners have put ourselves at the center. When we walk through the woods, we see what God has created. But when we drive around suburbia, we see what humanity has created. "We are making the world a place where the voice of God is muffled."[17]

This is increasingly the case as green space and parks disappear from suburban developments, as municipalities determine that the land has greater value when developed for commercial purposes. Cities continue to cut budgets for parks and public recreation facilities. In many areas, the only place for kids to play is in the commercial environment of fast-food restaurants. McDonald's is now the largest owner of playground equipment in America.[18]

Many of us intuitively have a clearer sense of God's presence through

In suburbia, we see what humans have made.
In the wilderness, we see what God has made.

his creation in nonurbanized areas. So as a spiritual discipline, it is helpful for us to escape the confines of suburbia every once in a while and experience the great outdoors, God's creation as minimally touched by human activity. It's not just that we experience nature in some utilitarian way in which we use it as a means to get closer to God. Rather, let nature remind you that God is concerned with the scope of all creation, not just our human concerns. Suburbia tells us that we are the center of the universe; God's creation reminds us that God alone deserves all glory and honor.

The psalmist calls everything *that has breath* to praise the Lord (Psalm 150:6). Concrete malls and asphalt parking lots don't have breath. But ducks and frogs and squirrels do. Even plants have respiration. Indeed, we wouldn't be able to breathe if trees and other green plants were not breathing in carbon dioxide and breathing out oxygen. In contrast, most of the human-made world has no breath, just ventilation. My coworker Sally lamented to me that our office building has no windows that can open. The building must be regulated for air quality control. It doesn't breathe. But the natural world, the trees of the field and the birds of the air, all that has breath, offers up worship and testifies to God's matchless worth.

Biologists and doctors have published numerous studies of the medical benefits of time in the outdoors. We are physical beings. Created in God's image, yes; but we are also members of the natural world of plants and animals. Our blood and tissues are as much a part of the created order as is the physical stuff of polar bears and mallards and groundhogs. Is it any surprise that we breathe deeper and feel more invigorated when we are in the outdoors, by a mountain stream or a seashore? The fluids in our bodies sense the rhythms of the tides. We feel the natural, God-created connections to the world around us.

When we go hiking or swimming we use our limbs and exert our muscles in very different ways than we do driving our cars or typing on keyboards. We experience a fuller physicality. I say this as a nonathlete. I have never been much for physical exertion, but I understand that when I go for a stroll in the park, I have a closer connection to the world God created than I do when I drive my car. Human beings were designed to walk and run and jump and move on the earth. We were not designed to be seat-belted into airplane seats for hours on end, which is why doctors encourage us to stretch and walk around the plane on long flights, lest we develop blood clots. We were not created to sit motionless in movie theater seats for two or three hours at a time, nor were we intended to spend our lives sitting in front of a television or video game console.

This is not to diminish the reality of our everyday lives, much of which is spent sitting at office desks or driving in cars. This is merely to recognize that these tend to be human-originated activities, not God-created activities.

On occasion we should fast from the structures and constraints of suburbia. To be reinvigorated by natural environments and pristine wilderness areas is healthy. But it's not merely that we have weekend getaways to the country to escape the rat race and be restored for the next week back at the daily grind. Nor is it just a utilitarian matter of using nature to find refreshment and refueling. If that's all it is, then we can easily come to depend on our escapes as ways to medicate our pain. Time away from suburbia should enlarge our hearts for suburbia and drive us back toward suburbia.

Time in the outdoors ought to reorient us toward the world that God has asked us to be good stewards of. Then we can find ways of enjoying and appreciating the natural world even as we live in suburbia. For some of us, gardening or yard work is an opportunity to enjoy creation, to touch the earth and sense the vitality and life that God brings through it. For others, caring for pets and the daily discipline of walking a dog are ways we see God's creative activity through the animal kingdom.

Care for creation includes respect for animal life. Francis of Assisi would pick worms off the road and carry them to safety. The Orthodox Church "forbids the harm of any creature—even insects—within the church. . . . The grace of sanctuary is extended even to life that cannot understand the One who provides it."[19] When I find insects inside our house, sometimes I kill them, but other times I try to scoot them outside and preserve their life. In some small way I feel that this honors the life that God has granted even the lowliest of creatures. In fact, to my wife's chagrin, sometimes I simply let such critters be, as a reminder to myself that I ought not imagine that I can ever purge my household of all non-human life. Indeed, nature and God's animal kingdom will reassert themselves and reclaim our territory after we are long gone.

We are part of God's creation, and something within us yearns to be in the midst of natural places and among plants and animals. I am reminded of this when my son tires of being cooped up indoors all day and asks to go outside to visit the ducks. It's a delight to walk to the park and watch bunnies scamper across our path. I once read about a study that tracked children's dreams and found that the number one thing kids dream about is animals. And why shouldn't it be so? Though we may dwell in the city, we retain primeval memories of life in the garden. It's part of who we are. And perhaps we best reflect our being created in the image of God when we dwell equally at home in garden and city, Eden and New Jerusalem.

A SUBURBAN SENSE OF PLACE

"We are used to having natural places, our mountains and rivers, appreciated as sacred places," writes Eugene Peterson.[20] We are not as accustomed to seeing human-made environments as holy places that God inhabits. God seems self-evidently present in the wilderness, where all creation declares his glory. We don't have as much of that sense of God's presence in the midst of asphalt and concrete. But should we?

I have almost always had a greater sense of awareness of God's presence when I have been standing on a lakeshore in the north woods of Minnesota or at a camp in the upper peninsula of Michigan or in the Rocky Mountains of Colorado. God somehow feels closer to me there than he does in suburban Chicagoland.

But part of me wonders if this is how it should be. Perhaps I have it backward. Shouldn't I have a clearer sense of God's presence in the midst of my daily environment? Shouldn't I be as able to pray at home as in the wilderness? I remember commenting to an acquaintance that I seem to be best able to pray and experience fellowship with God when I am somewhere away from my usual setting. He told me that he was exactly the opposite. He experienced God most often at home, in the midst of his daily routines, and he found that he struggled to maintain his relationship with God whenever he traveled. Being uprooted from his familiar places made him feel distant from God.

In an ideal world we would experience God's presence wherever we go, whether at home or away, in suburbia or in the wilderness. God is available to meet us no matter where we are located. But this isn't to say that we experience God the same way everywhere or apart from our physical context. We are embodied beings, and as such we never experience God in a vacuum. We always practice our spirituality in the context of a certain place. And places are not neutral. Different places give us different "vibes." Some places may seem more sacred to us, while others may be more secular or profane. And people will respond differently to particular locations. A place where God seems close and present to me may be one where God seems distant and absent to you, depending on your personality and temperament.

The ideal is to cultivate a spirituality of place in which God is experienced as real in more places than not. Psalm 139 reminds us that God is always present, regardless of place. In John 4, the Samaritan woman asked Jesus if the proper place of worship was in Jerusalem or Samaria, and Jesus responded that worship was not about a particular place but rather about an attitude of spirit and truth. So we need not travel to particular holy sites in order to pray or worship. We must not delude ourselves into thinking that God is more present in some scenic vista than in some suburban subdivision.

That being said, many factors prevent us from hearing God in the suburbs. Suburban environments are often filled with noise. If you close your eyes and listen carefully, what do you hear? If I am in my home, I hear the hum of the air conditioner in the summer or the furnace in the winter. If I am outdoors, I hear cars and trucks driving on a nearby road, perhaps airplanes flying overhead or lawnmowers down the block. I might hear the marching band practicing at the high school football field or music from a car radio. I will probably not experience much silence.

Solitude and silence are classic spiritual disciplines, and Christians have long extolled the virtues of quiet contemplation and creating space for us to hear the still, small voice of God. As Ruth Haley Barton puts it, "To enter into solitude and silence is to take the spiritual life seriously. . . . In silence we create space for God's activity rather than filling every minute with our own."[21]

Thus in our human-centered suburban environments, solitude and silence are profoundly countercultural practices. But they don't lead us to retreat from the world in some ascetic, hermitlike way. Henri Nouwen says that solitude, rather than isolating us from others, actually drives us toward community.[22] In solitude we experience the greatness of God and our utter dependency and insufficiency apart from him. In solitude, we are reminded not only of our own frailty and weakness but also of the needs of others. Thus, time spent in solitude sends us back to the human world, with hearts sensitized and more compassionate toward our fellow humankind.

We can experience God's presence both in his created order as well as in human society. We see glimpses of his kingdom coming and his will being done even in the midst of suburban environments. As one Latin hymn puts it: "Ubi caritas et amor, Deus ibi est" (Where charity and love are, there God is). When suburban neighbors reach out to one another in times of difficulty or grief, when friends delight in the simple joys of a backyard barbecue or an evening stroll, where children laugh and play and splash in puddles and blow dandelion seeds, in all of these God is present. We experience glimpses of God's shalom, life as God intended it to be, and we are at peace.

We need not flee the suburbs to really experience God. Nor can we appreciate God only in our suburban context. Suburban spirituality is not an either-or. The reality is more both/and. Suburbanites both need to get out of suburbia on occasion and also need to be fully present within it. God can thus be encountered either way.

PRACTICING THE PRESENCE

Too often I rush through my day, my mind filled with the multiple agenda items and concerns, with little space for contemplation or prayer. I then sit down at lunch or dinner, about to say a perfunctory "Thanks for this food," and I realize that I have not spoken a word to God or given him a thought all day. Even though I have a Christian worldview and identity, my daily life often resembles that of a practical atheist or a deist at best, lacking many signs of a dynamic, active spiritual life lived in the presence of God.

What can we do about this? The answer is not merely focusing on God during a brief, compartmentalized time slot and then racing off to the next activity. More significantly, I need to recognize God's presence throughout my day, allowing the inner witness of the Holy Spirit to direct my thoughts and activities in attunement to his voice. Christians have called this reflective mindfulness practicing the presence of God. As

Brother Lawrence's *The Practice of the Presence of God* puts it:

> When we are faithful in keeping ourselves in his holy presence, keeping him always before us, this not only prevents our offending him or doing something displeasing in his sight (at least willfully), but it also brings to us a holy freedom, and if I may say so, a familiarity with God wherein we may ask and receive the graces we are so desperately in need of. In short, by often repeating these acts they become *habitual,* and the presence of God becomes something that comes naturally to us.[23]

For me the most intriguing thing about practicing the presence of God is that it challenges me to see everyday activities in a new light. It infuses my ordinary habits with theological meaning and spiritual significance.

For example, in my morning routine, when I take my shower I might let the cleansing waters remind me of my baptism. Just as certain church services reenact and recall our baptism, showering can be an experiential reminder of God's forgiveness and washing away of sins, that his mercies are new every morning. As we begin the day physically clean and renewed, so too can we consider it a rite of spiritual cleansing and renewal.

Likewise, when I put in my contact lenses, I might pray, "Be thou my vision," and ask God for clarity of sight and insight this day. When I eat my bowl of cereal, I thank God for his provision and pray for those who do not have daily bread.

When I go around the house and gather the garbage and recycling, I use the act of taking out the garbage as a way to remind me to take the garbage out of my own life. As I go from room to room to pick up trash, I think through different spheres of my life and repent of various sins. Wednesday mornings when I put the garbage can and recycling bins out on the curb, I thank God that he removes my sins as far as the east is from the west, and I praise him for being the God who recycles, who takes the used-up parts of my life and brings renewal and new life to them.[24] Likewise, household chores, like cleaning and vacuuming, can take on spiritual significance if we use them as triggers for personal cleansing and confession or opportunities for reflection and prayer.

I also practice daily journaling every night before I go to bed. I've kept a journal regularly since high school, and I still use the same kinds of narrow-rule spiral notebooks and blue ballpoint pens I used back then. I have milk crates filled with dozens of notebooks chronicling the last two decades.[25] Some nights my entries are little more than, "Had a meeting with so-and-so today," or "Josiah pooped on the potty! Yay!" But even if nothing revolutionary or world-shaking happened, the mindful review of my day's activities helps me see where I saw God at work in my life. And the daily practice gives me a natural space to go to God on occasions that warrant more significant spiritual reflection, such as when I'm working through a crisis, processing grief or wrestling through an important decision. Journaling is a discipline that calls me to be honest with myself, God and others day in and day out.[26]

Another habit that many Christians practice is fixed-hour prayer, or praying the daily office. At particular times of day specific prayers are prayed and Scripture passages and other readings read. In a monastic setting these are done in community, but in modern suburban life we can pray and read by ourselves out of a book of hours.[27] There is great value in intentionally interrupting our daily life to acknowledge God even in the midst of our daily tasks.[28] Such prayer times can be triggered by preset alarms on one's cell phone or computer.

I personally have great difficulty practicing fixed-hour prayer, but that may be a reflection of my personality. I suspect that certain temperament types are more drawn to regular, systematic approaches to spirituality whereas others are more at home with other practices. We shouldn't be quick to prescribe one-size-fits-all approaches to spiritual practices, since different people naturally gravitate to certain disciplines as more helpful than others. Everybody's spiritual life will look different based on who they are and where they are at in life.

My interest in classical spiritual formation, practices and disciplines is a relatively recent development. I am a book geek, and I easily lose myself in abstract head knowledge. What are becoming more important to me are the concrete realities of such Christian practices as charity, hospitality, generosity and service. More than mere intellectual content, I need a healthy Christian spirituality where I am actively becoming more like Christ.

Most significantly, few of my suburban neighbors are very impressed by my theological or doctrinal head knowledge. But if my life shows Christian joy and contentment, hope and trust, faith and love, and spiritual health and life even in the midst of a secular, material world, then the gospel may well seem appealing and compelling. May we cultivate and practice Christian spirituality in such ways that God is indeed found in the suburbs, not only by ourselves but by those around us as well.

THE SUBURBAN CHURCH

Gathering Places of Relevance and Hope

The third place *is exactly what Willow Creek is attempting to be.*
Not home, not work, definitely not your father's church, but
something including all three.

JAMES B. TWITCHELL, *BRANDED NATION*

Suburbia is a challenging context for Christianity to take root in. The suburban forces we have explored militate against Christian community and identity in complex ways. But other comparable challenges face every environment and demographic region in the world. And every area has its own opportunities as well. Thus the prospects for the suburban church are both daunting and encouraging.

Sociologist Ray Oldenburg has argued that America is in need of more public "third places," apart from the first two places of work and home. More than ever, suburbia needs the church to be the third place. Suburban churches hold the potential for becoming third places where social capital can be re-created and people can reconnect with each other and with God. Churches can recover their historic identity as local community centers and gathering places. Such churches can both connect with suburbanites where they are at but then call them to a different kind of suburban life.

I am not a pastor or professional church consultant, so the following observations aren't meant to be taken as programmatic tools for crafting the ideal suburban church. Dozens of books have been written on how to lead and grow a healthy church, and I will not duplicate their work here. Rather, what follows are diagnostic markers of some of the challenges and opportunities facing the suburban church.

THE CONTEXTUALIZED CHURCH

During college I did a summer internship at a church in my suburb. Though I had never attended this church, I sought it out because it was affiliated with my college. Because it was nearby, I was able to live at home during the summer. It was a congregation of about a hundred people and was in a prime location, near the middle of town at a very visible intersection just off one of the main highway ramps.

Over the course of the internship I noticed something about the church's ethos. It didn't feel like other suburban churches in the area. On the contrary, it reminded me of other churches in the same denomination that I had visited in rural areas. I wasn't able to put my finger on what it was that made it feel different, but in contrast to other churches that had grown up in that community, this church didn't feel contextualized to its suburban environment. It was also much smaller numerically, despite its convenient location, and not very well known or influential.

I later learned that this particular movement of churches began the American frontier, primarily in rural, small-town settings. When the movement planted churches in urban and suburban settings, they often retained the flavor of the small-town church. In fact, because of shared architectural plans and templates, some suburban congregations have the exact layout and décor as their small-town counterparts, even if the architectural style of the surrounding neighborhood is entirely different. Many members are transplants from small towns looking for continuity with their rural church experience. These churches thus tend not to attract their suburban neighbors.

My theory is that churches like Willow Creek Community Church in suburban Chicago or Saddleback Church in suburban Orange County have become successful megachurches not merely because of their seeker-sensitive approach but because they have astutely contextualized their ministries, programs and even their architecture to a suburban environment. They live and breathe the suburban air in such a way that suburban residents feel fully at home in their buildings and worship services. They are comfortable seeing themselves as suburban churches ministering to suburban people.

Churches like Wooddale Church in suburban Minneapolis have intentionally copied the architecture of suburban shopping centers and parking lots. In fact, "Wooddale" parallels the names of nearby suburban malls like Southdale and Rosedale. Leith Anderson, senior pastor of Wooddale, wrote this about his church's architectural design:

> Wooddale Church sought to incorporate many of the architectural features people experience in schools, office buildings, and shopping centers. The building must seem comfortable to those who have never gone to church before. There are large halls, shopping-center-type parking lots, contemporary interior decorating, disabled access, user-friendly signage, Coke machines, gymnasium, commercial kitchens, and modern offices. The symbols and story match the people of the community.[1]

At the same time, Wooddale looks like a church. It has a steeple and a cross, and in its sanctuary, its giant pipe organ is prominently visible. It doesn't look like a generic community college or community center. In short, the church had contextualized itself to fit its suburban environment without being religiously neutral.

On the other hand, the leadership of Willow Creek Community

Church intentionally designed their church to look like a community college or community center. In 1975 twenty-three-year-old Bill Hybels went door-to-door in the community to ask people if they went to church, and if not, why.[2] What he heard convinced him that there were untold numbers of people who would never darken the doors of a traditional church. From the very start, Willow Creek was infused with a passionate commitment to understanding unchurched suburban residents and ministering in ways that would resonate with them. They didn't want anything, even good Christian imagery or architecture, to become a stumbling block to prevent people from attending. Thus Willow Creek has no crosses or steeples. Its auditorium evokes the feel of a community theater or concert hall rather than a cathedral.

Willow Creek has been criticized for its lack of religious imagery and design. But perhaps Willow Creek is designed to be more attractive to people from unchurched backgrounds who do not feel comfortable in church buildings, while Wooddale is more clearly a church for suburbanites intentionally looking for a church. Generic meeting places, like high schools, may be better for those who have been wounded by church experiences and have visceral psychological reactions to being in church buildings. But others have a residual longing for the religious significance of transcendent worship in a building that evokes historic church architecture.

My own sense is that I prefer a church to look like a church. If a church can be mistaken for an office complex, it is dependent on signs or its members to draw visitors. But if its very architecture somehow indicates the presence of the sacred and its purpose in worship, then the building itself collaborates with its body in witness to the community.

Whatever form a church's architecture takes, more important is that a congregation's ministries, activities and worship services are contextualized to its suburban setting. What might that look like?

THE CHURCH IN A COMMERCIAL CULTURE

Suburbia is the natural habitat of both the shopping mall and the mega-church, and the two share more than a family resemblance. While mega-churches are neither the most numerous kind of church in suburbia nor found only in suburbia, the synergy between megachurches and suburbia is worth examining because they have contextualized themselves to suburbia's commercial environment.

Willow Creek Community Church took its name from the Willow Creek movie theater it once met in. Advertising and branding expert James B. Twitchell observes, "Rather like malls that take their name from what they destroy, so this church takes the name of the entertainment it now competes with."[3] Visitors to megachurches like Willow Creek drive long distances, park in vast parking lots, eat at the food court, shop in the bookstore, and watch video and music presentations while sitting in auditorium seating. The kids can be dropped off in secure childcare. The programming is well-produced and entertaining. While the content is Christian, the form is thoroughly suburban—commuter, consumerist, convenient and media immersive.

Twitchell points out that megachurches have co-opted four major systems from malls and entertainment complexes. First, megachurches use music much as shopping malls or Starbucks do; there's a soundtrack to the experience that you can buy to take home with you. Second, large visual screens replicate a moviegoing or sports-arena Jumbotron experience. Third, huge parking lots, complete with parking attendants, ensure commuters an efficient experience. Fourth, childcare doubles as both convenience for harried parents as well as programming to create future generations of megachurch-branded loyalists.

As megachurches multiply their ministries, they may inadvertently perpetuate a consumerist mindset. Both mall and megachurch "offer a panoply of choices under one roof—from worship styles to boutique ministries, plus plenty of parking, background music, clean bathrooms, and the likelihood that you'll find something you want and come back."[4] Mall marketers have identified a phenomenon called the "Gruen transfer," named after Victor Gruen, architect of Minnesota's Southdale mall. Having similar stores in close proximity increases consumption at all of them. You plan on buying something at one mall store but then wander into another next door or down the hall and pick up other things you had no idea you wanted to get.

How does the Gruen transfer apply to churches? "As we consume in clusters, so too do we worship," says Twitchell.[5] A church with myriad ministries from support groups to aerobics classes to basketball courts to marital counseling creates a mini-mall effect. You come planning just to worship, but afterward you pick up a cup of coffee and drift into the bookstore and buy a sermon tape and a book or worship CD. The church as one-stop shop for activity and consumption substitutes for the suburban shopping and entertainment complex. It embodies the suburban tendencies to be more, do more and consume more and more.

It is now quite common to drive by older strip malls and see signs not for Toys "R" Us or Kmart but rather Community Fellowship Church and Victory Christian Center. "One of the primary redevelopers of derelict malls around the country has been the megachurch. Old shopping meccas are becoming new religious meccas."[6] This may be savvy missiology, presenting the church in a sociological context already comfortable to the suburban consumer. Worshipers may not even need to move their car between worshiping Sunday morning, eating at a restaurant at noon and picking up some groceries that afternoon.

Churches have long been in the business of schools and daycares, but many have diversified their businesses to provide different avenues for reaching different potential attenders. Some churches actually have national chains operating in their food courts. Robert Putnam notes that

> Southeast Christian Church in Louisville, Kentucky, and Brent-
> wood Baptist in Houston, Texas, have built facilities that are in ef-

fect church-centered malls or small towns, with health clubs and athletic facilities, McDonald's franchises, banks, and other amenities designed to attract people and encourage them to eat, play, and work as well as worship there.[7]

Some churches run diners or fitness centers. Many have banqueting and catering services. Some have video arcades. Some even have crematoriums. "These seemingly unthreatening churches are becoming a parallel universe, a self-conscious branded community, social magnets drawing in all manner of outside services."[8]

The upside of this is that it gives such churches myriad opportunities to become all things to all people. The downside is that the megachurch becomes dependent on competitive amenities, just like any corporate, commercial entity. The unintended consequence of such pragmatic ministry is that it perpetuates a consumer Christianity where people simply shop for the church with the best deal and the most attractive conveniences and offerings. Little heard is the prophetic word that might inconvenience the attender or dissuade the customer.

One way to see this is that consumer society has co-opted the church. Another way to see it is that Christian faith is reclaiming certain spheres of daily life. Is this contextualization or compromise? Like all our efforts in an imperfect world, such ministries are likely a mix—tainted by the Fall yet pursued with hopes of redemption.

THE CHURCH AS CIVIC CENTER

Some suburban megachurches have come to achieve a distinct sociological function. They fill the suburban vacuum with their own religious version of public square and city center. Twitchell's description is worth quoting at length:

> A megachurch often behaves like a successful mall, consolidating other frayed institutions such as school, family, government,

neighborhood, and even employment. In a sense, a megachurch mimics the Norman Rockwell town center, complete with the town square—the commons. Having people milling around is crucial. By taking on roles as various as those of the Welcome Wagon, the USO, the Rotary, the quilting bee, the book club, the coffee shop, and the country club mixer—and, of course, the traditional family and school—these "next churches" have become the traditional villages that many Americans think they grew up in and now can find only on television.[9]

In other words megachurches are the contemporary fulfillment of small town and urban life in a suburban setting. They provide the critical mass and structural framework for the community life lacking in most suburban areas. In this, ironically, they are both countercultural and completely contextualized at the same time. There is nothing more suburban than a megachurch, precisely because it is providing everything that suburbanites long for but can't find in suburbia.

"The megachurch is at this intersection between sacred and profane. It inspires reverence, awe, and commitment and at the same time it attempts to generate a mimic of village life."

JAMES B. TWITCHELL, *BRANDED NATION*

Suburban churches can offer a certain degree of civic good when they provide alternative third places for church and community groups to meet. All churches can be used as public meeting places. While few churches have food courts or espresso bars, most have fellowship halls and meeting rooms that can be used for civic community gatherings, not just church events. Girl Scout troops, Weight Watchers, Al-Anon and a whole host of other community organizations can all meet at the neighborhood church rather than at the VFW or Starbucks.

In previous generations many churches were always open so community members could use them as public meeting halls. They may not have even had locks on the doors, which communicated that the church was always available to any who wanted to enter. These days, security concerns have often closed churches off to their local neighborhoods. Perhaps churches can reverse this trend and open their doors to community events and gatherings. They can serve as public polling places on election days. They can host nearly any kind of community group, formal or informal, from knitting groups to neighborhood watch meetings. If you participate in local community activities, suggest meeting in your church building. Make the church a natural meeting place for the community. Instead of only launching new ministries to attract people to the church, investigate what other community organizations and networks could be invited to meet in your church building.

On the flip side, many churches already meet in public or semipublic third places, such as schools, community centers, fitness clubs, restaurants, theaters or coffeehouses. Not having buildings of their own, these churches provide natural opportunities to encounter newcomers precisely because people are already coming to these places. National Community Church in Washington, D.C., meets at a movie theater in Union Station, four blocks away from the Capitol building. Pastor Mark Batterson says, "Our strategy is to be in the middle of the marketplace, to take the church where the people are instead of trying to get them to come to us."[10] They are now planting churches in movie theaters near train stops around the metropolitan area. They have also purchased a building that they are renovating into a coffeehouse. They don't own a traditional church building; instead their only building is strategically intended to serve as a connection space in the hub of the nation's capital.

Multisite church Community Christian Church of Naperville, Illinois, has a satellite congregation that meets in a community center in the outlying suburb of Romeoville. One Sunday morning a local resident showed up in his gym clothes, basketball in hand, to discover some sort of meeting set up in the gym. Intrigued, he sat in the back row with his basketball under his chair and stayed for the service. The church was talking about getting to know people in your neighborhood, and the man signed up for a small group. A few months later he and his brother both became Christians. Pastor Dave Ferguson says, "This is a perfect example of how the third place helps us fulfill our mission, which is to help people find their way back to God."[11]

CHURCH COMPETITION

The United States is a spiritual marketplace because of two major factors: the First Amendment's freedom of religion, and the absence of a state church. The democratic nature of American government is reflected in our churches. While elsewhere on the planet you can find the Church of England or the Church of Scotland, there is no Church of America or, for that matter, a Church of Illinois or Church of New Mexico. Instead we have the American Baptist Churches, the Evangelical Lutheran Church in America, the Orthodox Church in America, the Presbyterian Church (U.S.A), not to be confused with the Presbyterian Church in America or all the rest. The very geography of America's vast land mass means that religious communities had the space and freedom to found new churches and denominations. The lack of a state church, combined with Protestant denominationalism, created a free-market atmosphere for churches. And as a result, people choose churches much like they choose any other commodity—by shopping.

Freedom of choice and religious pluralism may actually bolster local congregational commitment and allegiance. The very fact that multiple kinds of churches are available can enhance and deepen church commitment. Sociologists Rodney Stark and Roger Finke studied the link between religious diversity and church commitment. They found that "in towns of similar size, church attendance was highest when there was the greatest choice of worship. In short, brand commitment varies directly with choice: the more variations, the deeper the affiliation." In marketing terms, "Competition often increases consumption."[12] In a democratic society, consumers resist monopoly and prefer a marketplace of choices.

The danger is that in such an environment, people tend to choose churches that only suit their predispositions and preferences. Think of how viewers watch cable television. The people who watch the Sci-Fi Channel or Comedy Central are generally different kinds of people than those who watch the History Channel, the Biography Channel, A&E or public television. Cable channels narrowcast rather than broadcast their programming to attract a particular niche of viewer.

In fact, networks not only try to attract their desired viewer—they also consciously or unconsciously work to repel undesirable viewers. Communications professor Joseph Turow gives the example of MTV's animated program *Beavis and Butt-Head*. Not only did this show clearly signal who its audience would be (primarily males ages eighteen to twenty-five), it also repelled virtually every other demographic. Elderly women and soccer moms were not going to be tuning in to this show. Such a show had the effect of purifying MTV's audience, so it could tell its advertisers that they were sure to deliver the desired viewership. Turow cites the *Los Angeles Times*'s assessment: "Say what you will about the moronic duo, they've helped to cement MTV's identity with viewers and advertisers."[13]

Think of what happens when you turn the radio dial, looking for a station you want to listen to. If you don't like country music or hard rock, you will continue to dial past stations playing songs in a genre. But if you hear a familiar tune from your teen years, whether that was during the 1960s or 1990s, chances are you will stop and listen for a while. The very nature of music preferences is that music attracts its own tribe of listeners and repels others.

Translate this principle to the world of suburban Christianity. In a marketplace of churches, different churches attract certain demographics and repel others. Each church has its own brand identity, for good and for bad. Some churches by their very nature attract young single twentysomethings, while others attract middle-aged parents of tweens and teens. Some will attract liturgical worshipers and repel contemporary worshipers, and others vice versa. Most churches tend to not be all things to all people; they will usually be one main thing and attract a certain kind of person.

When churches think about contextualizing their ministries to their suburban context, it is not enough to ask "What is the community like?" They must also ask "What are we called to be?" It is entirely appropriate for different churches in the same local area to have entirely different styles of ministry and worship. If each is true to its distinct calling, heritage and identity, each will attract and minister to a distinct kind of person that the others are not as likely to connect with. Ray Bakke writes, "Because the city is so pluralistic, we need every single denomination, ministry-style and model. One is not better than the other, any more than a bus is better than a car. It depends on the task to be done."[14]

A diverse suburban culture includes many subcultures, so a community will naturally need a variety of churches to reach different kinds of people. The danger, of course, is that people will tend to gravitate toward a particular kind of church that reinforces their own sense of identity, and there may be little diversity within a particular congregation. The body of Christ has many parts, both on a micro and a macro level. And we are impoverished if our Christian community is largely homogenous.

What happens when an individual's sense of Christian calling and vocation seems to be at odds with his or her home church? A church may be very strong in children's ministry or personal evangelism but may lack ministries in social justice. A parishioner called to social justice can stay at that church and become an advocate for justice issues, or he or she can gravitate toward a congregation that already embodies those values and is active in justice work. Sometimes this may degenerate to a mere matter of preference for the pastor's preaching or musical worship style, which may not be legitimate reasons to change churches. But the ultimate question is one of vocation. What kind of Christian is God calling you to be? And what kind of church is your church called to be?

In many cases, God may call you to belong to a congregation that you never would have chosen. The denominational background, liturgical style or "brand identity" may be completely at odds with what you may have ever thought to belong to. But local church bodies, like the universal body of Christ, are diverse and complex entities, and God may well be shaping you in surprising ways at a church where you don't seem to fit in.

We shouldn't choose a church in consumerist ways. Rather, we ought to attend a church on the basis of discernment and submission to Christian community and identity. For some of us proximity might be the defining issue, and thus we go to the church closest to our home. For others our distinct Christian identity as a Baptist or Presbyterian or Anglican might be the most important factor. We don't just shop for the church with the coolest worship team or the best children's programs; we worship and have fellowship on the basis of submission to a particular Christian community or tradition.

Small churches need not try to compete with the bigger churches that have the resources to do dozens of ministries. It may be more realistic for small churches to do one or two things particularly well. The business book *Good to Great* profiled companies that were the best in the world in a particular dimension or industry. What can your church be best at in your community? Are there one or two areas of focus that can make you distinctive? There may be a dozen churches in a particular suburb, but only one might have a counseling ministry, a grief ministry, a support group for recovering from chemical addictions, or a mothers of preschoolers group. Given your particular theological heritage, denominational emphases and mix of members' giftedness, identify the particular ways your church can minister to your community in ways that no other church can. Embrace your particular identity and be who you are called to be, and you will attract those who are called to be part of your congregation, even if your style runs counter to what the successful megachurches look like.

THE COUNTERCULTURAL CHURCH

It's not enough for suburban churches to contextualize themselves to their suburban environment. They must also simultaneously try to offer a countercultural Christian alternative.

Eugene Peterson argues that "when you start tailoring the gospel to the culture, whether it's a youth culture, a generation culture or any other kind of culture, you have taken the guts out of the gospel."[15] He tells the story of how his son, Eric, planted a new church. It met in a high school auditorium, and Eric wore business suits rather than clerical robes, for fear of turning off unchurched people skeptical of religious imagery.

When Advent rolled around, Eric felt that he just needed to wear his robe. Eric's neighbor Joel came to visit the church. "Joel was the stereotype of the person the new church development was designed for—suburban, middle management, never been to church, totally secular." After the Advent service, Eric asked Joel what he thought of his wearing a robe.

"It made an impression," Joel responded. "My wife and I talked about it. I think what we're really looking for is sacred space. We both think we found it."[16]

This kind of prophetic, countercultural sense of sacred otherness can get lost when suburban churches overly focus on felt needs, inadvertently feeding into a cult of self-centeredness where the gospel is merely a vehicle for self-improvement. Peterson identifies the danger of "advertising the faith in terms of benefits" as "exacerbating the self problem." All of us have met certain kinds of people, he says, who are tremendously "spiritual" and love God, pray and read Scripture. But all they think about is themselves, Peterson points out. They wonder, *How can I*

witness better? How can I do this better? How can I take care of this person's
problem better? The self-centered perspective is subtly disguised because
the spiritual talk disarms us.[17]

Is there any way to escape this? After all, churches ignore their parishioners' needs at their own peril. Peterson's point is valid if a bit over-
stated. Clearly, there is value in having ministries and support groups to
meet such felt needs as helping people find healing from addictions,
abuse or divorce. As a starting point a church can incarnationally contextualize itself to seekers' needs and meet them where they are at. But
that is not all. It should also take them beyond cultural norms to experience a prophetically countercultural way of living the Christian life.

The challenge is to avoid creating a subculture in which the person's
Christian involvement and identity is framed in terms of Christianity's
benefit to the individual. At some point in the spiritual formation process a degree of Christian maturity should lead us to live and serve and
be Christians not because it makes our life better but because this is the
life to which we have been called, for better or for worse. We do a dis-
service to unchurched seekers when we invite them to come to Jesus because he will make their lives better. That may be the case, but it may
also be the case that Christianity will involve incredible suffering and
pain. And that is just as much a part of following Jesus.

Churches must be both incarnational and countercultural, and it's always tricky to walk that line between the two. One critique of contemporary seeker churches is that though their intent is to make church accessible to the unchurched, an unintentional side effect is to dechurch
the churched. If a church contextualizes itself too much to emulate a secular suburban culture so suburbanites feel comfortable visiting, it may
very well lose its Christian distinctiveness. Church loses its sacredness.

This is why during the same recent decades that contemporary megachurches have blossomed, many have also gravitated toward the liturgical, ancient-future renewal in church and worship. It's a recovery of the

sacred, of a divine otherness, of glimpsing God in ways that aren't seen in the rest of daily life. Religious imagery, symbols, rituals, liturgy, "smells and bells" are increasingly being rediscovered, especially by younger and emergent generations, as an antidote to the secularity of the era. Such practices are no longer the turnoff that previous generations of church consultants once thought they were.[18]

When my wife and I left our previous seeker-sensitive contemporary church to move into a liturgical Anglican one, I e-mailed our former pastor and told him, "My take on ecclesiology allows me to affirm that you are helping your church become the church that it is called to be, even as we seek out the church that we are called to be a part of." Whatever identity a church is called to have, no church is perfect, nor can be, nor needs to be. All will attract a certain kind of worshiper and repel others. If your church is contemporary and seeker-oriented, maximize your opportunities to reach the unchurched, but beware the temptation to be too felt-need and self oriented. If your church is more traditional, maximize your distinctiveness and continuity with the past, but beware the danger of becoming irrelevant and distanced from the surrounding culture and community. Either way, churches are called to be both incarnational and countercultural, in ways that fit their calling and identity.

One distinct way suburban churches can be countercultural is to create space for quiet and reflection. A recurring refrain in suburbia is that everybody is too busy. Those who move to the suburbs from small towns usually say that the pace of life is faster and that it's harder to have meaningful time with other people. There's little time for church involvement or ministry because there's just not enough time in the week to get everything in.[19] Weekends are filled with detailed itineraries of things to do and places to go. Stores are open 24/7, so errands are done on Sunday afternoons between church and youth group. There's little time to relax or to have any sense of sabbath rest.

Countering this reality of modern life, some youth pastors are creating alternatives to traditional youth ministry events. Many teens are so frazzled by all the activities of the week that the last thing they need or want is to have more crazy activities and games at church. So these youth ministries take the opposite approach. Instead of more things to do, youth group consists of quiet spaces, with darkened rooms and a few lit candles where teens can come and experience silence and rest. Instead of more go, go, go, they instead are invited to simply be and rest, to pray and to listen, to let God minister to them in the midst of silence and solitude. The pace of suburban life is such that teens (and their parents) are starving for this kind of contemplative spiritual experience and countercultural encounter with God.[20]

CHURCH CLOSE TO HOME

In chapter three I raised the topic of recovering a parish concept, where we seek to live, work, shop and worship all within a particular community. If you sense God's call to be more intentionally a part of your local community, you may seek out the church closest to your home. If you are committed to your church but live far away, you may sense a call to relocate closer to your church.

We can learn from the example of Orthodox Jews. Many Orthodox Jews live within a one-mile radius of their synagogues. Why? Because they can't drive on the sabbath and must live within walking distance. Jewish historian Etan Diamond points out, "For members of this group one question usually supersedes all others when moving households: is it near an Orthodox Jewish synagogue? If not, then that particular place will get crossed off the list, no matter how nice, affordable or convenient it might be."[21]

Throughout the mid-twentieth century, a few hundred thousand Orthodox Jews transformed certain local suburbs by concentrating their housing in particular areas. This affected local commerce, public schools and civic life, creating a distinctly Jewish subculture where Jewish ethics and religious values infused the community. "The Orthodox Jewish community saw suburbia as a neutral environment capable of being transformed into a religious landscape," writes Diamond. "In moving from city to suburb, Orthodox Jews literally broke new ground by spatially separating themselves from the old neighborhoods and choosing to become religious pioneers on the suburban periphery."[22]

If Orthodox Jews could create religious community in suburbia, why not Christians? What might it look like for Christians to have such a sense of sacred suburban space? What would a church's neighborhood look like if a significant percentage of its members lived in a one-mile radius? For one thing, more members would have a sense of investment in that local community. Some churches have youth groups where teens attend as many as eighteen high schools because their families are scattered across a region. If the entire youth group went to the same high school, they could have a greater critical mass and missional impact there.

Unfortunately, many churches are commuter congregations where most attendees live far from the church's local neighborhood. Many churches no longer have parsonages, so even the pastors might live several suburbs away from the church building. If few people in the church live in the physical neighborhood where the church is located, the church will have a difficult time being truly incarnational.[23] Just as urban churches call their members to relocate to revitalize an urban neighborhood, so too a suburban church could call its members to move into particular communities or subdivisions to maximize the church's ministry impact there.

There are signs of resurgence of such localism. Catholic parishes still hold that people should worship and take Communion in their local parish. And evangelical megachurches and metachurches are creating multisite and satellite ministries, with local congregations for local communities. Over one thousand churches in North America are now multisite churches.[24] The multisite church seeks to bring the church closer to its members' homes. Rather than ask parishioners to commute to a central location, the church looks at where its members live and starts local gatherings in those areas.

Community Christian Church in Naperville, Illinois, is one of the pioneering examples of the multisite church.[25] It is one church in five locations. It has a main central campus but also other sites in areas of new suburban growth. Each site has its own pastoral staff, worship team and small group ministry, so congregants stay local and worship with people in their own municipality. Some worry that this may become franchise-like, but it's a way to have local affinity and yet continuity congregationally over a more widespread metropolitan area.

IN SEARCH OF A SUBURBAN CHURCH HOME

During summers home from college I attended a megachurch in the Minneapolis suburbs that drew six or seven thousand every weekend. It had never used any formal evangelistic program; twelve years prior it was just an ordinary congregation of about 150 people that suddenly took off. It met in a high school gym and had high-energy worship and dynamic preaching, with a significant commitment to worldwide missions. It was located about half an hour away from my home. I made the drive just to see what was so compelling about it, and I was hooked. Even after I went back to college, I subscribed to their worship tapes and sermon tapes so I could replicate some of that megachurch experience. I was thrilled with this church; it resonated with me as a suburbanite. It was cool to be able to say that I went there.

The downside? I never connected with anyone. I made no friends there. I would visit and bring friends with me, and we would marvel at the church's vision and vitality. But even though every worship service had a greeting time when we were exhorted to introduce ourselves to people around us, I never met the same person twice. I occasionally ran into somebody I knew from high school, but for the most part I stayed anonymous. As a transient college student I was not able to get involved beyond casual attendance. It's no mistake that megachurches constantly encourage their members and visitors to get plugged into small groups; the mantra is that as a church gets bigger, it needs to get smaller.

I moved to Illinois for graduate school, and there I connected with a church of about nine hundred attendees. It was less than a mile from where I was living, and it had intentionally contextualized its ministry and architecture to fit the local community. It was a very vibrant contemporary congregation with fully orbed ministries and missions work, and I quickly felt at home. I got plugged in, made good friends and became active on the leadership team of the singles ministry. But I only spent time with other people in the same demographic as myself, single twentysomethings without kids. It still seemed like too big a church for me to get to know other kinds of people.

After I got married, my wife and I found a church close to our new apartment, one that averaged about 250 in attendance each Sunday, small enough for us to get connected and contribute. Ellen and I got involved primarily in the worship ministry but also in other spheres of the church, and we experienced a greater cross section of ages and backgrounds than folks like us. Due to energetic young leadership, the church grew and expanded to over four hundred regular attendees.

After about seven years at this church, Ellen and I began to sense that we were being tugged in a more liturgical direction. So we moved to a new church, a tiny Anglican church plant just a few months old with less than fifty people. Even though it had far fewer resources or programs, and our son Josiah was one of just four or five kids in the children's ministry, the distinct sense of evangelical Anglican identity and contemplative spirituality was so compelling that we knew we had found our home. Our son Elijah was the first baby born in the life of the congregation.

All four of these churches are suburban churches—the megachurch, the big church, the middle-sized church, the tiny church plant. Are any of them the ideal suburban church? No, each has its own advantages and disadvantages; each has particular strengths and weaknesses. Yet each heralds the kingdom of God in its own way, and suburbia needs all of them.

Our church transitions have been a gradual progression in our Christian pilgrimage. I don't mean to imply that church hopping is a legitimate way of life. Our experience of community life is impoverished if we don't practice stability and have longevity with a local congregation. As we have discerned a clearer sense of who we are and how God is forming us, we have sought to bring our personal identity in alignment with our church identity. But spiritual journeys will differ, and some may change churches over the years while others are called to stay in the same congregation for decades.

Ultimately, church is less about us shopping for our needs and more about being formed as God intends for us in our particular station of life. It's less important that a church is using the latest ministry techniques and more important that a church is being what God has called it to be. There is no deep knowledge of God without deep knowledge of the self, and there is no deep knowledge of the self without deep knowledge of God.[26] In the same way, the more that suburban churches and parishioners alike come to a deeper knowledge of the true selves that God is calling them to be, the more we will become the churches we are meant to be, and the more we will all be able to live out our sense of vocation and calling.

Beyond Suburbia

Mission to and from the Suburbs

The suburban congregation has a moral responsibility to the life of the entire metropolis.

Gaylord B. Noyce, *The Responsible Suburban Church*

Most of this book has been about understanding suburbia on its own terms and considering how Christians might seek to live out our faith in a suburban setting. But it isn't enough to live in a suburban bubble, isolated from a larger context, both immediate and global. For all our efforts to work and live and witness and minister in suburbia, we may only grasp God's call to seek the shalom of the city when we look beyond our suburban environments.

The summer before my senior year of high school, I went on a short-term urban mission trip to inner-city Minneapolis. For two weeks we were immersed in the realities of social injustice and disadvantaged neighborhoods, poverty and crime, homelessness and addiction, racialized inequalities and structural decay. We volunteered with a youth center, served meals at a soup kitchen and distributed food at a community pantry. Our host pastor lived next door to a crack house, and the local police had used the pastor's upstairs bedroom as a vantage point for a stakeout.

It was a jarring environment, and our team of mostly rural and suburban teens wrestled with our own prejudices and misconceptions. Many had never been in a setting where white people were in the minority. While we were never really in harm's way, some of our guys were hassled and roughed up by local youths. Over and over we were confronted with the questions: What would Jesus do here? How would Jesus minister to this neighborhood? What is the good news of the gospel for these communities? We learned that spiritual comfort about God's love, inner peace and eternal life was not enough. Christian ministry encompasses whole persons and communities: Bible studies and gospel tracts were meaningless without sheltering abused women and children, feeding the homeless, and working toward economic and social justice.

What was most convicting for me was the fact that we were working in inner-city neighborhoods only about ten miles away from my suburban home. I lived in the *very same county,* but I had never ventured into the depths of the 'hood. I had driven by on highway bypasses countless times, but I had never met these people, let alone considered them my neighbors.

Seeing the reality of urban need activated my faith and challenged me to move beyond being a Sunday Christian. While I have since done ministry work in other contexts, both domestic and overseas, that first urban experience had the most lasting effect on me precisely because it was geographically so close to home. No longer could I consider myself just a resident of Bloomington, the individual suburb. I needed to reckon myself a resident of the Minneapolis-St. Paul metropolitan area. I came to understand that my county was home to both million-dollar mansions and crack houses. I could no longer say that the problems of inner-city Minneapolis were none of my business. It had become part of my world. I needed to broaden my sense of citizenship and ownership and consider myself part of a larger reality.

SUBURBAN-URBAN INTERDEPENDENCE

A suburb tends to be a place "with a certain psychological distance from the city proper, a sense of being 'out there' instead of 'in there.' "[1] This psychological distance is more significant than any geographic distance. Even if a suburban church is only five minutes or five miles away from an inner-city community, it might as well be across the country or halfway around the world. Indeed, many suburban churches give more to overseas missions than they do to support local ministries in nearby urban centers.

It is common shorthand to speak of suburbs and cities in opposition or at least contrast, but they are interconnected components of a larger urban reality. A study by the National League of Cities showed that "although urban losses sometimes create short-term suburban gain, they almost invariably hurt suburbs in the long term."[2] Our destinies are intertwined. Suburbanites and urbanites together must affirm that to care about one requires that we care about the other.

Indianapolis mayor Stephen Goldsmith worked with suburban officials to share infrastructure and regional transportation planning in ways that would benefit both the city and the suburbs. He writes, "Suburban businesses and residents must understand the need for the regional economy to expand together, and that today's edge city will be threatened tomorrow if the concentric circle of poverty and despair continues to grow."[3] In other words, suburbanites cannot only focus on their own immediate suburban concerns. The economic and social destinies of cities and suburbs are inextricably related. Even as suburban centers grow in self-sufficiency and prominence, they depend on a larger metropolitan ethos of health and stability.

How can suburbanites influence the wider metropolitan context? Robert Putnam, author of *Bowling Alone,* argues that rebuilding social capital in civic community takes two dimensions. First is *bonding social capital,* the internal community bonds and relationships within organizations. This happens within churches when members relate to one another, meet in small groups and the like.

But bonding social capital is not enough. The second dimension is *bridging social capital*. "Whereas bonded capital is the strength *within* a social segment of society, bridging capital is the strength *between* the segments of society."[4] Communities must not only build bonds within; they must also build bridges without. This is an area where evangelical churches have traditionally been weak. Sociologist Robert Wuthnow writes, "Mainline Protestant churches encourage civic engagement in the wider community, whereas evangelical churches apparently do not."[5]

Church consultant Eric Swanson calls churches to be outwardly focused and to "measure their effectiveness not merely by attendance but by the transformation effect they are having on their communities." He writes:

> As churches partner with people in neighborhoods, schools, human service agencies, business and government agencies, they are creating bridging capital within these neighborhoods, not just by linking the entities of a neighborhood to the church but helping to link the entities to one another. It is the church's care and love that build bridges through tutoring programs, ministering to the battered women in the safe house, hosting job fairs and opening day care facilities. As churches seek to be agents of community transformation, they should not ignore their abilities to bring social capital to a community—building community bonds and community bridges.[6]

Healthy suburban churches will see themselves as an integrated whole with the larger metropolitan area, both suburban and urban. While they may have a specific calling to minister to their immediate, local suburban community, that ministry should be seen in the context of overall metropolitan mission.

Naturally, no church can do everything. But every church can do something. Different churches will be called to different ministries as determined by the makeup of the congregation and particular denominational or theological emphases. Some churches have a long tradition of championing social justice issues and care for the poor. Other churches emphasize evangelistic ministry and Bible teaching. Communities need both. A community with a mix of churches with many emphases can minister holistically to both the spiritual and physical-social needs of the metropolis.

Just as most local churches partner with particular missionaries and mission organizations around the world, so too can local suburban churches likewise partner with urban ministries and organizations in nearby cities. Theologian John Schneider calls this the principle of "moral proximity."[7] We are naturally most concerned with those closest to us—our families, neighbors, coworkers and fellow church members. But moral proximity does not mean that we are *only* concerned with those immediately before us; that would be insular and narcissistic. So I listen to Chicago Public Radio, read the *Chicago Sun-Times* and think of Chicago news as affecting me and speaking to the issues of my metropolis. It isn't enough to only concern myself with suburban Downers Grove; metropolitan Chicago must also be on my horizon.

INTENTIONAL PRESENCE

The apostle Paul's missionary strategy was to go to the urban centers. Throughout the book of Acts he visited such cities as Corinth, Athens, Ephesus and ultimately Rome. But what passed for a big city in those days would be considered relatively small today. Some of today's midsize suburbs are larger than Paul's urban centers.[8] Paul's metropolitan strategy, if applied to our modern context, would likely see him traveling to urban and suburban areas alike.

Rich Lamb, in his book *Following Jesus in the "Real World,"* describes the usual postcollegiate pattern of life.[9] College graduates usually find a job somewhere and move to wherever they can find affordable housing. If they're Christians, they'll then visit various local churches and make one of them a church home. They'll make friends in that church, and may eventually get involved in some sort of ministry through that church, using their gifts to serve others.

In this pattern the *job* is the lead factor. It sets everything else in motion. This is actually the opposite pattern of what we see in the book of Acts. The apostle Paul on his missionary journeys always traveled with a group of friends. They went to various cities to start churches. In other words, there was intentionality both in first gathering the Christian community and then in selecting a local community to live in. They moved into an area with their core group of Christian cohorts already present with them. They ministered to that area. And their jobs, whether tentmaking or leatherworking, were incidental; they were just something that they did to support themselves.

What would it look like if Christians got together and decided to move to an area and minister to it without worrying about their jobs? Instead of the job being the lead factor, how about having the community be the decisive factor? That might also cut down on transience. Usually people relocate because they get a better job offer, so they uproot themselves and figure they can start over and find new friends, churches and ministries elsewhere. What would it look like if we prioritized the friends, churches and ministries we now have rather than the jobs that would take us away from them? Choose your community, live there, work there, worship there and minister there.

Of course, some people are comfortable with a life on the move, at least for a particular season of life. Younger people, especially singles and those without children, are more free to relocate wherever jobs, relationships or mission opportunities may take them.[10] Some are called to an itinerant lifestyle, going wherever God may send them. Certainly there is biblical warrant for this. Jesus himself was constantly on the road, and

Paul's missionary journeys took him to various cities for a few months or years at a time. So there is a missionary aspect to the Christian life, and we must be open to going wherever God may lead us.

On the other hand, some of us need to hear the call *not* to go but rather to *stay.* Frequent moves diminish our ability to have established, credible witness in a community. We can't get involved with the school district or befriend neighbors if we're only there a year or two before moving on. So if possible, try to remain in a local neighborhood for an extended period of time. Don't think in terms of just the next year or two but the next five, ten or twenty. If you have young children, don't consider their elementary school only but their high school as well—and envision the thriving Christian fellowship group they could be in by the time they get there. If one doesn't exist, consider what you might be able to do between now and then to make that dream a reality.

Consider the possibility of sensing God's calling for a particular community. Sometimes a job transfer or career change requires a relocation, but if you are merely changing housing, see if you can remain in your local community for as long as possible. We are called to be good neighbors to our communities, and we can't do that well if we are nomads and frequently uprooting ourselves.

God needs suburban Christians who are willing to take a sharp look at their environment, recognize the challenges of the suburban setting, and then *stay here* to do something about it. Some Christians live in suburbia because it is a fulfillment of their personal American dreams for comfort and prosperity. Others are here only out of necessity and would gladly move away at the drop of a hat. Some love it here, some hate it. Many are indifferent. But whatever we may feel, for whatever reason we came, as long as we are here, the call is the same: Seek the welfare of the suburb you are living in.

What does that mean? That will mean different things for different Christians, since all of us have different passions, gifts and callings. For some, seeking the welfare of the suburb will mean civic involvement, serving on the school board, volunteering for community events. For others, it will mean neighborhood evangelism. It could be tutoring troubled youth, befriending single parents or serving hidden disadvantaged populations, like the homeless or displaced refugees. This may involve your local church, or it may be a ministry done on your own. But the call to seek the welfare of the community is distinctly nonprivatistic. It calls us out of our suburban isolationism and anonymity. It exhorts us to come face to face with neighbors and strangers. It asks us to seek the good of others outside our own homes.

Christians are called to *transform* the suburbs, just as we are called to transform every area, every community, every place it is possible to live in. We can celebrate and preserve the good things that suburbia does well, and critique and challenge the fallen, broken places that yet need kingdom transformation. And because of metropolitan interdependence, transforming suburbia may well transform urban and global sites both near and far.

DISPLACEMENT

Some Christian mission leaders challenge young people to give up their lives and dreams of "suburban affluence" in order to serve God overseas or in the inner city. Such appeals may be effective and well-intentioned, but can be a bit oversimplistic: Suburbia = bad. Anywhere else = good. Such dichotomies are no longer adequate. Suburbia is as much a part of God's global mission as any other part of the earth. God is raising up a generation of people who will be strategic mission agents in whatever area of the world he sends them—whether rural, urban or suburban, domestic or overseas.

One of the hallmarks of the Christian community development movement has been relocation into underserved and underprivileged neighborhoods. This strategy has had significant transformative impact.

While many suburban Christians are unwilling or unable to relocate into needy areas, many could, especially as older first-ring suburbs come to resemble urban environments. God needs Christians everywhere, suburban and urban alike.

Whatever our starting point, we should be open to the Christian practice of *displacement*. Henri Nouwen writes that in displacement, "as a Christian community we are people who together are called out of our familiar places to unknown territories, out of our ordinary and proper places to the places where people hurt and where we can experience with them our common human brokenness and our common need for healing."[11]

Displacement is a biblical pattern. God's people have always been called to go to unexpected places, whether as pilgrims or exiles. Jesus is our ultimate model of displacement; his incarnation demonstrates the extent to which he was willing to displace himself on our behalf. When Jesus told Peter that he would someday go where he did not want to go, he was declaring to all succeeding generations of Christians that in following him, the way of displacement is the way of the cross.

If we live and serve in suburbia, we must not let inertia prevent us from hearing God's call to go elsewhere. Displacement will often take us to places of greater need and brokenness. Thus we should carefully consider opportunities to follow Jesus to disadvantaged communities in urban and global settings. But displacement does not flow in only one direction. Displacement is not always a major visible lifestyle shift like moving to an urban neighborhood. Displacement doesn't necessarily mean dislocation. Indeed, Nouwen says that "we must begin to identify in our own lives where displacement is already occurring. We may be dreaming of great acts of displacement while failing to notice in the displacements of our own lives the first indications of God's presence."[12] For many Christians, living in suburbia is itself an act of displacement. Likewise, many of our suburban neighbors are themselves displaced, and our presence in the community can be a ministry of welcoming the stranger, refugee and alien.

We may find ways of practicing displacement even within a suburban environment. We can join churches with different ethnic, racial or economic demographics, or seek out ministries to disadvantaged populations. Our friends Ted and Alexis felt called to live in an ethnically and economically diverse community, and they considered moving to a more urban setting. But Ted's job was in a suburb, and they wanted to live as close to his work as possible to avoid unbearable commutes. So they intentionally moved to a neighborhood in a nearby suburb with a higher percentage of people from different ethnic, linguistic and national origins.

However we experience displacement, above all else "voluntary displacement can only be an expression of discipleship when it is a response to a call—or, to say the same thing, when it is an act of obedience."[13] Even if suburbia is only a temporary stop for you on your life journey, the Christian call is to live Christianly in suburbia as long as you live in suburbia. Faithfulness within suburbia enables us to take larger steps of displacement later. As Nouwen says, "The more we are able to discern God's voice in the midst of our daily lives, the more we will be able to hear him when he calls us to more drastic forms of displacement."[14]

A THEOLOGY OF BOTH OCCUPATION AND ENGAGEMENT

Urban community developer Robert Lupton, in his book *Renewing the City*, tells a story that sheds light on how we might have better Christian presence in our communities. He consulted with an urban church that had challenged its suburban members to move into its local, disadvantaged neighborhood. The church responded with surprisingly strong commitment and enthusiasm, and over a course of several years, nearly 250 members moved into the immediate neighborhood.

Lupton was amazed. He asked the pastor, "So what has happened in the community?" The pastor replied that they had started a number of programs, including after-school tutoring, English as a second language classes, a counseling ministry to single moms and even a community development corporation.

Lupton was impressed. But he still wanted to know—"What is happening in the community?" The pastor seemed confused. He repeated the list of programs.

"Yes, but what is happening in the community?" Lupton asked. To clarify what he meant, he asked, "Has crime gone down? Has drug trafficking dried up? Has prostitution left? Has the education level improved in the neighborhood schools?"

"No, not really," the pastor admitted. People were being helped, but many of their converts weren't coming to church. The church was trying to figure out if there were ways to be more hospitable and welcoming to people of different racial and ethnic backgrounds so they would be more likely to enter into the life of the church. While there was some influence and change in individual lives, as a whole the church still had little impact on the systemic and structural problems of its inner-city neighborhood.

"Then it dawned on me," Lupton writes:

> These were suburban Christians, born and bred in individualism, who had brought with them into the city a church-centric theology of personal salvation and corporate worship. Ministry to the poor—ministry to anyone—was evangelism driven. A vision for the rebirth of a community could only be understood through the lens of saving souls and adding to the church rolls. The reclaiming of dangerous streets, the regeneration of fallen systems, the transformation of corrupted political power—these were aspects of God's redeeming work in the world that had somehow been omitted from their biblical teaching.[15]

As suburbanites we must beware the temptation to think of mission only in terms of Western individualism, "changing lives one by one."

While we must never neglect the significance of evangelizing individuals, equally important is transforming societal, organizational and municipal structures. It's not enough to assume that converting individuals will eventually lead to those individuals making their communities better on an individual basis. It's one thing to try to convert public officials one at a time and disciple them so their policies are more just. It's another to organize a community to enact systemic change that will better the entire community, regardless of whether or not the policymakers or the residents are yet Christians.[16]

Whether we are ministering in suburban or urban contexts, our mission must be incarnational as well as invitational, with a holistic understanding of God's kingdom transforming all of society, not just the individuals within. Besides our concern for our lost neighbors, we must also be concerned about fallen social systems, unjust legal codes, inadequate infrastructure and public services, community welfare and harmony.

"The church's ministry in the world involves concern for both the individual and the culture. The two are inseparable."

GAYLORD B. NOYCE, *THE RESPONSIBLE SUBURBAN CHURCH*

"A theology of occupation is a huge step in the right direction, but it is not enough," writes Lupton. "It must be coupled with a theology of engagement—an understanding of how the people of faith are to engage in activities that transform places as well as people."[17] Having a theology of occupation, in which Christians enter into and establish a significant presence in a particular community, is not enough, especially if they are only present with the intent of befriending and evangelizing neighbors. A critical mass of Christians must also be engaged with the community and seek ways to change societal ills, just as William Wilberforce's suburban community of Christians banded together in Christian activism to abolish slavery.

The Bible describes "cities of refuge" that served as places of asylum where people could be protected from vengeful retribution. A theology of occupation and engagement would help us consider how our cities and suburbs might likewise become places of refuge and safety, where the poor and needy are provided for, basic human needs are met, and people have fruitful work and shared community life. Implicit in such a vision is that we must know our community's needs and participate in its community life to work for the common good.

A GOSPEL OF BOTH SALVATION AND STEWARDSHIP

Old Testament scholar Walter Brueggemann has articulated a distinctively balanced and comprehensive gospel of shalom for both the poor and the rich, the haves and the have-nots. One major theme in biblical history, especially the Old Testament, is deliverance for the oppressed. Many parts of the prophetic record were addressed to people in precarious positions who cried out for rescue and salvation from slavery, from opposing armies, from unjust rulers. In these situations God's message of shalom was one of deliverance and salvation for the have-nots. This is the gospel we are most familiar with; we apply it to the alcoholic or addict who finds freedom from his addiction, the wayward prodigal who returns to faith, the sick and dying who are restored to health and life. Whether applied to physical or spiritual needs, the gospel is undoubtedly one of deliverance and salvation.

But this is only one side of the story. Brueggemann demonstrates that another strand of the biblical tradition is framed for the wealthy, the affluent, the haves. He writes:

> People who are well-off have very different perceptions of life and a very different theological agenda from those who must worry about survival. Both are in the Bible, and while church theology has taken the *Bible's theology of survival* seriously, it has been less perceptive about the *Bible's theology of management and celebration.*[18]

When life is not precarious, when survival is not at stake, the gospel is not one of deliverance but rather of "proper management and joyous celebration." The poor and oppressed need to hear God's word of salvation and rescue. The rich and well-off need to hear God's word of stewardship. It has often been said that God comforts the afflicted and afflicts the comfortable. Brueggemann would say that a biblical theology of shalom is a gospel of deliverance for the oppressed and stewardship for the blessed.

The stewardship tradition comes out of times in Israel's history when the kingdom was at peace, and good kings and rulers sought to manage their kingdoms justly, blessing their people with the fruit of God's goodness. They didn't need to rescue them from any immediate threats; rather, they were good stewards of the bounties that God had provided and sought to administer and distribute the resources equitably. The wisdom literature arose out of this tradition; Proverbs is much more concerned about wise management of resources than deliverance from tyranny.

The gospel of salvation and deliverance is good news for the poor and oppressed. It means that God is calling them out of Egypt, out of slavery, out of sin and death. The gospel of stewardship and celebration is good news for the well-off and secure. It means that God is calling them to be his stewards and to responsible, wise management of his good resources, so that they and others can experience the blessings of his shalom.

These two dimensions go together; in fact, they are two sides of the same coin. Indeed, there is overlap between them, and many Christians will experience both aspects of this gospel over the course of their lives. Some start from a position of deliverance from dire straits and are rescued from self-destruction and eventually move toward a place of stewardship and blessing toward others. Other Christians may first understand God as the source of great blessings and only gradually understand that he is also the savior who delivers them from evil.

For many affluent suburban Christians the challenge is to discern ways to live out this gospel of stewardship and blessing. We are familiar with the story of God's rescue and redemption; we are more uncomfortable with the call to be stewards of God's blessing. The biblical concept of shalom is that of wholeness, peace and security, life the way God intended it to be.[19] A gospel of deliverance provides the first half of the equation—moving away from life as it is not intended to be. A gospel of stewardship seeks to fill out the second half—moving toward a life of wholeness and shalom, so that people and communities live and thrive as God intended. The salvation gospel deals with fall and redemption. The stewardship gospel goes back to creation and envisions consummation.

Brueggemann's doesn't pit the two approaches against each other; indeed, they are complementary. Police officers and firefighters, for example, may on occasion rescue victims from danger (salvation and deliverance) but also work to maintain order and peace (stewardship and management). Most middle-class suburban Christians aren't in precarious positions, though we have plenty of anxieties. So our gospel must be creational as well as redemptive; that is, not only do we affirm that God will make the wrong things right, we also affirm that much is right with the world already, and God entrusts us to extend those good creational blessings to others.

One suburban Christian told his pastor, "I am making way more money than I ever thought I would. I have way more than I need. What should I do?" Such are the dilemmas of the Christian wealthy. Is making money okay? Yes, when it is done purposefully and selflessly. As John Wesley put it, Christians ought to make all we can and save all we can so we can give away all we can.

When faced with the poor and disenfranchised, some Christians could share wealth and resources to meet their needs, and other Christians could join them in solidarity and incarnationally share their experience. It's not a simple switch of rich Christians becoming poor. Some rich Christians ought to give away all they have and become poor—if that is God's call to them. Others may be led to do what they can to acquire wealth so that those resources can be used strategically for the benefit of the worldwide church. In other words, rich and poor Christians together must collaborate for the furtherance of the kingdom of God. One can't say to the other, "I don't need you!"

Some of us may be following Christ by giving up lucrative careers to serve with the poorest of the poor. And others of us may be following Christ by working on Wall Street or Capitol Hill, in strategic places of power and wealth, in order to direct resources to the needy. God works through Christians in all places.

If we are affluent suburban Christians, we can be like Joanna, one of the wealthy women who underwrote Jesus' missionary work. As the wife of Herod's steward, she likely had significant assets. She and others provided resources for Jesus and the disciples so they could travel and minister. Following Jesus meant that she used her wealth responsibly, not for her own self-interest but for the benefit of Jesus and the extension of the kingdom. Likewise, the money that we spend consuming can be used instead as resources to bless the nations and fund urban and global ministries. The call to stewardship is one of gratitude for what we have received; we can then joyfully release it for the benefit of others. It's better to think of ourselves more as conduits of blessing rather than reservoirs or banks where resources are hoarded. We have been blessed so we can bless others.

If you are a suburban Christian, you must determine what kind of suburban Christian you are going to be. Will you be virtually indistinguishable from your neighbors, consuming and commuting and striving and acquiring like everyone else? Or will you live out a missional suburban Christianity, where you are connecting and giving and sharing and practicing hospitality, generosity, community and self-sacrifice? If we are suburban Christians with access to wealth and power, we must wield that power responsibly. If we are in positions and places of privilege, we need to steward those resources and deploy them strategically and freely.

GLOBAL CONCERN

When I was in 4-H as a kid, I pledged my head, heart, hands and health to service for my club, my community, my country and my world. I now hear in that 4-H pledge echoes of Jesus' call to Jerusalem, Judea, Samaria and the ends of the earth. Wherever we may be, we inhabit all those varying spheres and concentric circles. We may be suburbanites, but we are also citizens of a larger, global urban population. And as such, we must seek the welfare of the whole world.

This can be a bit overwhelming. I am still figuring out what it means to be part of the particular suburban community of Downers Grove. I have hardly begun to grasp what it means to consider myself a citizen of Chicago. But I am learning to have a wider, missional perspective on matters both local and global.

For example, most of us don't think of ourselves as either rich or poor. We think of ourselves as middle-class, comfortable but not ostentatious. But in global perspective we are incredibly rich. If we have a blanket and a pillow, we are rich. If we have two shirts, we are rich. Untold millions around the world live on less than a dollar a day. In America "the average household headed by someone with a college degree has an income of about $72,000 a year. If you live in that household, you are richer than 95 percent of the people on the planet. You are probably richer than 99.99 percent of the people who have ever lived."[20] Given our extraordinary access to wealth, a theology of stewardship calls us to find ways to release our resources for the benefit of the global church.

When youth groups and church teams go on short-term mission trips, they often come back saying that they were ministered to more than they ministered. At best, this is a humble acknowledgment of experiencing and receiving God's grace in unfamiliar settings; at worst it can be a narcissistic self-centered focus. Even if mission teams didn't "accomplish" very much overseas, they are very often transformed and newly motivated to live out their faith back at home. Urban or overseas mission trips can awaken us to the needs of the world. Even if we don't pursue a lifelong vocational ministry in impoverished areas of Bangkok or Nairobi, we may return with a far more serious commitment to living out the Christian life in the suburbs we call home.

The horizon of suburban life can blind us to the AIDS epidemic in Africa or genocide in Sudan or sex trafficking in Malaysia. These kinds of global problems seem so far removed in scope and distance that we don't know what to do about them. So we end up dulling our hearts and ignoring news reports. What can we do?

Let me suggest some baby steps. A well-rounded Christian should be involved at some level of ministry in at least three spheres: immediate community, most likely via one's local church; wider regional ministries with a metropolitan scope; and overseas missions or ministry efforts. Our ministry concerns ought to encompass the suburban, the urban and the global.

At the local level we can be involved with the particular neighborhood or suburb that we inhabit and seek out ministries and ways to embody Christian love and faith to our geographically closest neighbors. Local community clothing closets, crisis pregnancy clinics, homeless shelters, Alpha courses or divorce care ministries are but a few of the possibilities. Then we should be involved with a ministry that takes us beyond our immediate area, perhaps to nearby regional urban centers. Concern for the wider urban metropolis may mean that we become involved with community development or parachurch organizations with influence in public policy, higher education, or media and culture. And for an international, global perspective, we could support overseas efforts ranging from Bible translation and church planting to sponsoring children or stopping sex trafficking or genocide.

I am not too concerned with the particulars of what individuals, families and churches might do, since I trust that the many varied members of the body of Christ will find ministries and outreaches suited to their particular interests and callings. My main concern is that we lift our eyes beyond our immediate environment and never fall back on the excuse that we were too busy with our local issues to care about the rest of the world. One person can't do everything, but all of us can do several things. And if we can do our best to seek the welfare of both our local communities as well as others across the country and around the world, then our energies will be better balanced and our vision will be clearer.

It's impossible for us to do something about every global problem, but we may be called to do something about one or two issues in particular. A suburban Christian high school of 575 teens rallied around a vision for fighting AIDS in Africa, and in three years they raised nearly $250,000, enough to build a medical clinic and a schoolhouse and provide a year's supply of food for a village in Zambia. It was almost entirely funded from the teens' own pockets, as they encouraged one another to give up movies, Starbucks coffee, Christmas presents and prom dresses. Students then visited Zambia to see the fruit of their efforts and came away with both a greater sense of partnership as well as new ideas for funding, like a maternity ward. They have also launched AIDS Student Network, with a vision to recruit a thousand American high schools to combat AIDS in Africa.[21]

Part of the discernment process is to identify what specific things God may want you to claim as your own. Research some options online, consult with your church's missions ministry, and then prayerfully pick one or two that particularly resonate with your sense of calling and concern. You could free child prostitutes by supporting the work of International Justice Mission or support disaster cleanup efforts through World Relief. You might send shoeboxes of Christmas gifts through Samaritan's Purse's Operation Christmas Child. You can sponsor a child through World Vision or Compassion International. If you are a medical professional, you might naturally get involved with health care efforts in the developing world. Our family has found great joy in partnering with ministries in global justice issues, whether providing resources to free a child from slave labor or contributing transportation for disabled refugees.

Peggy Wehmeyer, host of *World Vision Report*, realized that her children had gotten spoiled and were demanding unreasonable Christmas presents. So she and her husband revoked their presents and instead gave them gift catalogs of missional gifts they could provide to needy children around the world. (Many Christian missions organizations have catalogs where you can order shelters for disaster relief, a goat or cow for a family, medicine for treating AIDS and the like.) They gave each of their daughters a budget and a choice. "Here's how much we'd normally spend on you," the Wehmeyers said. "We'd like you to think about giving one of your gifts away to one of these kids."

Both girls took the task seriously. After looking through the catalogs, Lauren compiled a long list of all the things she wanted to order for other kids. "But honey," Peggy said, "If you get all that, you'll use up your budget." There would be nothing left over for her.

"That's really what I want to do, Mom," Lauren replied. "These kids need so much. I don't need anything."

That Christmas, even though there were no brightly wrapped packages under their tree, Peggy said, "the best gift was the one my husband and I received—seeing our girls turn into young women who would choose compassion over self-indulgence."[22]

Whatever you end up doing, having global horizons reminds us that we are part of a universal body of Christ. Having a heart for our brothers and sisters in other places of the world may well help us have compassion for and openness toward those in our own suburban neighborhoods. We can likewise steward our suburban resources to bring blessing to larger urban and global concerns. And by God's grace, may his kingdom come and his will be done, in suburbia and the uttermost reaches of the earth.

Epilogue

Seek the Welfare of the Suburbs

Seek the welfare of the city where I have sent you into exile,
and pray to the LORD on its behalf, for in its welfare
you will find your welfare.

JEREMIAH 29:7

When all is said and done, how has suburbia shaped my worldview and Christian experience? As a product of suburbia I have been far more individualistic and self-autonomous than I ought to be. My experience of community is fairly weak. I am fragmented and anonymous. I am largely disconnected from the natural world of God's good creation. I tend to view life through the lens of consumer culture, and every action and decision is made with self-interest and consumption as the unconscious default setting. I am insulated and isolated from the needs of the world.

But not all is lost. Suburbia is also the crucible for me to learn the Christian disciplines of self-denial, simplicity and generosity. I am challenged to grapple seriously with the responsibilities of Christian stewardship. I am invigorated by the opportunities to create new forms of community and to practice friendship and hospitality. I am learning to counteract the lies of secularism and consumerism, even as I find ways to champion God's passions for peace and justice. In embracing my suburban context and loving my suburban neighbor as myself, I am rediscovering God's continual call to care for others both here and beyond.

In short, I am learning how to live as a Christian, regardless of my location. It strikes me that the things I am called to practice here in suburbia are the same Christian distinctives of love, witness, mercy and justice that all Christians should embody wherever they may live. There is truly nothing new under the sun, but we are called to live Christianly for such a time as this. The path of Christian discipleship is costly no matter where we are, but we have Jesus' assurance that he will walk with us wherever our journeys take us.

Suburbia is a place of spiritual impulses and longings—the desire for security, a place to call home, a healthy community, meaningful relationships and purposeful living. The suburban Christian not only finds these spiritual longings fulfilled in Christ and the Christian community, but also seeks to help others realize the fulfillment of these longings, ushering them into the blessings of the kingdom of God. We will ultimately move from a self-centered suburbanism that only looks inward and gratifies the self to a Christian other-centered suburbanism that looks outward and seeks to bless the nations. The redeemed suburban Christian can in turn become an agent of transformation not only for suburbia but for the world at large.

Whether suburban Christians consider themselves in paradise or in exile, God calls us to seek the welfare of the suburbs—to do what we can so others may experience the fullness of God's peace and shalom, life as God intended it to be. If we do so faithfully, we may find that God enlarges our hearts not only for our immediate neighbors but also to embrace his global, worldwide mission. And the suburbs may in fact become a foretaste of the heavenly city.

Go with God. Be not afraid. And I leave you with this Celtic blessing:

May the peace of the Lord Christ go with you,
    wherever he may send you.
May he guide you through the wilderness,
    protect you through the storm.
May he bring you home rejoicing
    at the wonders he has shown you.
May he bring you home rejoicing
    once again into our doors.[1]

ACKNOWLEDGMENTS

I do not so much write a book as sit up with it, as with a dying friend.
During visiting hours, I enter its room with dread and sympathy
for its many disorders. I hold its hand and hope it will get better.

ANNIE DILLARD, *THE WRITING LIFE*

Thanks to the many people who helped remedy this book's many disorders. As a result, as Monty Python might say, it got better.

Thanks especially to all those who read the manuscript, both officially and informally. The feedback was tremendously helpful and a humbling reminder that even editors need editors.

It truly takes a village to publish a book, and I am profoundly grateful to my colleagues in the village known as InterVarsity Press. Thanks to all of you for making our suburban scriptorium a delight to work at. Inestimable appreciation goes to publisher Bob Fryling; editorial director Andy Le Peau; acquiring and developing editor Cindy Bunch; managing editor Allison Rieck; editors Jim Hoover, Dan Reid, Dave Zimmerman, Gary Deddo, Drew Blankman and Joel Scandrett; proofreader Lisa Rieck; editorial assistants Elaina Whittenhall, Kristie Berglund and Taryn Bullis; transcriptionist extraordinaire Gloria Duncan; production director Anne Gerth; art director and cover designer supreme Cindy Kiple; book layout specialists Gail Munroe and Maureen Tobey; senior buyer Jim Erhart; production experts Lorraine Caulton and Audrey Smith; creative services maestros Rebecca Larson, Matt Smith and Mark Smith; webmaster Sally Sampson Craft and Web editor Else Tennessen; sales and marketing director Jeff Crosby; sales and marketing pros Greg Vigne, Andrew Bronson, Emily Varner, Darcy Wright, Heather Mascarello, Betsy Conlin, Peter Mayer, Marsha Barnish and Ruth Curphey; publicity divas Krista Carnet, Brooke Nolen and Jenny Locklear; call center heroes Kim Brown, Meya Starkey, Celeste Mirkovic, Scott Linhart, Kimberly Johnson, Cathy Bradley and Victor Rivera; financial and accounting gurus Jim Hagen, Julie Isenberger, Nancy Bucklin, Dave Page, Judy Hessel, Florita Lopez, Nadine Hunt, Ron Lee, Carey Aten, Scott Griffith, Holly Brauch and Samantha Miller; IS tech wizards Ron Lanier, Andy Shermer, Tricia Koning and Brian Cody; receptionist Audrey Ward; executive assistant Stacey Weber; general services manager Arnold Young and his trusty sidekicks Ruth Davies and Dave Montei; distribution center commandos Doug Secker, Mike Zeman, Holly Shermer, Alan Platt, Bob Klopke, Monica Ly, Charlie Mikesell, Richard Dunn, Rob McKenzie, Jen Yahoudy and Jason Young; former colleagues Jim Connon, Judi DeJager, Jim Luedtke, Ruth Goring, Kristi Reimer, Denise Picard, Roni Smith, Candi Sauerman, Rick Franklin and Andrew Craft; and above all, the world's most efficient and splendiferous rights manager, Ellen Hsu.

Thanks also to our church family at Church of the Savior in West Chicago, Illinois, especially to our rector and deacon, the pastoral staff couple of Bill and Linda Richardson. We've been thrilled to join you on this new adventure of a suburban church plant. May we all continue to become closer friends of the Savior.

Finally, thanks again to my beloved wife, Ellen, and our wonderful kids, Josiah and Elijah. Okay, Josiah, you can play on the computer now—I'm done.

NOTES

Introduction

[1]David Brooks, *On Paradise Drive* (New York: Simon & Schuster, 2004), p. 48.

[2]Rosalyn Baxandall and Elizabeth Ewen, *Picture Windows* (New York: Basic Books, 2000), p. 236.

[3]Margaret Green, letter to the editor, *Christianity Today*, September 2003, p. 15.

[4]Rick Halvey, letter to the editor, *Christianity Today*, September 2003, p. 15. Ironically, the same issue of *Christianity Today* had an article about cowboy churches that have contextualized themselves to a country and western setting, using country music in worship, wearing cowboy hats and boots and the like. This is considered good missiology. But suburban churches that embody their suburban environment are described as shallow and compromising themselves to the culture. Why not see suburbia as a similarly legitimate mission field?

Chapter 1: The Suburban Moment

[1]For example, "the city of Atlanta saw its population grow by twenty-three thousand over the last decade, but the surrounding suburbs grew by 1.1 million" (David Brooks, *On Paradise Drive* [New York: Simon & Schuster, 2004], p. 2).

[2]According to urban sociologist J. John Palen, in the last quarter of the twentieth century, "North America has gone from being a continent of city dwellers to a continent of suburbanites. . . . There has been a suburban revolution that has changed suburbs from being places on the periphery of the urban core to being the economic and commercial centers of a new metropolitan area form. Increasingly, it is the suburbs that are central with the cities being peripheral" (J. John Palen, *The Suburbs* [New York: McGraw-Hill, 1995], p. 1).

[3]Ibid., p. 4.

[4]Brooks, *Paradise Drive*, p. 3.

[5]Kenneth T. Jackson, *Crabgrass Frontier* (New York: Oxford University Press, 1985), pp. 5-10.

[6]Joel Garreau, *Edge City* (New York: Doubleday, 1991), pp. 4-5.

[7]Alex Marshall, *How Cities Work* (Austin: University of Texas Press, 2000), p. 66.

[8]Ibid., pp. 72-78.

[9]"The suburban periphery has become the favored locale for our most advanced and important enterprises. If anything, suburbia has succeeded too well. It has become what even the greatest advocates of suburban growth never desired—a new form of city" (Robert Fishman, *Bourgeois Utopias* [New York: Basic Books, 1987], p. xi).

[10]Dolores Hayden, *Building Suburbia* (New York: Pantheon, 2003), p. 11.

[11]Palen, *Suburbs*, p. 92.

[12]"From its first building boom in the late nineteenth century, Los Angeles has been shaped by the promise of a suburban home for all. The automobile and the highway when they came were no more than new tools to achieve a suburban vision that had its origins in the streetcar era. But as population spread along the streetcar lines and the highways, the 'suburbs' of Los Angeles began to lose contact with the central city, which so diminished in importance that even the new highways bypassed it. . . . By the 1930s Los Angeles had become a sprawling metropolitan region, the basic unit of which was the decentralized suburb" (Fishman, *Bourgeois Utopias*, pp. 15-16).

[13]Garreau, *Edge City*, p. 3.

[14]Robert D. Lupton, *Renewing the City* (Downers Grove, Ill.: InterVarsity Press, 2005), p. 126.

[15]William H. Hudnut III, *Halfway to Everywhere* (Washington, D.C.: Urban Land Institute, 2003), pp. xii-xiii. Some four hundred suburban communities in the study had an estimated poverty rate of over 20 percent.

[16]Haya El Nasser, "Small-Town USA Goes 'Micropolitan,' " *USA Today,* June 28, 2004, pp. B1-2.

[17]Robert Lang, in ibid.

[18]See Jackson, *Crabgrass Frontier,* p. 12.

[19]"Suburbs housed only 15 percent of the nation's population in 1920, and by the end of World War II only 20 percent of the United States' population resided in suburbs. . . . In 1950 a quarter of the United States' population lived in metropolitan-area suburbs. A decade later the figure had increased to a third of the nation's population, equaling that found in the central cities of metropolitan areas" (Palen, *Suburbs*, p. 2).

[20]Jackson, *Crabgrass Frontier,* p. 17.

[21]Palen, *Suburbs*, p. 22.

[22]Jackson, *Crabgrass Frontier,* p. 8.

[23]Lupton, *Renewing the City,* p. 126.

[24]One interesting aspect of American civic development is that cities were not nec-

essarily established first and had suburbs grow up around them. In many cases, multiple settlements were established in a state or region, and often one or another became dominant over its nearby rivals because of such factors as transportation infrastructure, commercial investment, political clout or civic leadership. "In effect, 'winning' towns came to form the nation's urban centers and the also-rans became their suburbs" (Tom Martinson, *American Dreamscape* [New York: Carroll & Graf, 2000], pp. 22-23).

[25]For more detail on this, see Ray Bakke's *The Urban Christian* (Downers Grove, Ill.: InterVarsity Press, 1987) and *A Theology as Big as the City* (Downers Grove, Ill.: InterVarsity Press, 1997); and Harvie M. Conn and Manuel Ortiz's *Urban Ministry* (Downers Grove, Ill.: InterVarsity Press, 2001). A wonderful portrait of Nehemiah as urban developer is found in Lupton's *Renewing the City*.

Chapter 2: Living in Suburbia

[1]C. S. Lewis, *The Great Divorce* (New York: Touchstone, 1996), p. 20.

[2]James Hudnut-Beumler, *Looking for God in the Suburbs* (New Brunswick, N.J.: Rutgers University Press, 1994), p. 2.

[3]William H. Hudnut III, *Halfway to Everywhere* (Washington, D.C.: Urban Land Institute, 2003), pp. 24-26, 28.

[4]Rosalyn Baxandall and Elizabeth Ewen, *Picture Windows* (New York: Basic Books, 2000), p. 125.

[5]Ibid., p. 256.

[6]Hudnut, *Halfway to Everywhere*, p. 29.

[7]Dolores Hayden, *Building Suburbia* (New York: Pantheon, 2003), p. 7.

[8]Tom Martinson, *American Dreamscape* (New York: Carroll & Graf, 2000), p. 242.

[9]Baxandall and Ewen, *Picture Windows*, p. xxi.

[10]Joel Garreau, *Edge City* (New York: Doubleday, 1991), p. 4.

[11]J. John Palen, *The Suburbs* (New York: McGraw-Hill, 1995), p. 89.

[12]While the majority of the population lives in cities and suburbs, in many minds, the ideal remains rural. One study found that while 77 percent of the population lives in metropolitan areas of over 100,000 people, only 23 percent say they want to live in areas that large. This seems to be a remnant of our frontier and pioneer mindset, where the homestead in the wilderness is still enshrined as the model. Over half of us live in metropolitan areas of over a million people, but only 2 percent (and declining) actually live on farms. Even those who say they want to live in rural or small-town settings still would prefer to live within thirty miles of a big city (ibid., pp. 94-95).

[13]Robert Fishman, *Bourgeois Utopias* (New York: Basic Books, 1987), p. 207.

[14]Palen, *Suburbs*, p. 89. This might seem self-evident, like dog owners having a pref-

erence for dogs or viewers of the Sci-Fi Channel preferring science fiction. But this is more than a lifestyle choice, considering that many people don't have the economic freedom to relocate to a different living environment. Economic forces have in many ways determined who can afford to live in suburbia.

[15]Hayden, *Building Suburbia,* p. 4.

[16]Ibid., p. 17.

[17]Ibid., p. 4.

[18]See Robert Bruegmann, *Sprawl: A Compact History* (Chicago: University of Chicago Press, 2005), pp. 97-98.

[19]See George Yancey, *Beyond Racial Gridlock* (Downers Grove, Ill.: InterVarsity Press, 2006), pp. 91-92.

[20]Dan Chiras and Dave Wann, *Superbia!* (Gabriola Island, B.C.: New Society, 2003), p. 12. Palen notes, "One of every three blacks living in a metropolitan area is a suburban resident. This is well beyond tokenism. African American suburbanization is substantial and widespread. Today, black suburbanism is a social reality; it is not simply a footnote to white suburbanization" (Palen, *Suburbs,* pp. 116-17).

[21]Baxandall and Ewen, *Picture Windows,* p. 240.

[22]Hayden, *Building Suburbia,* p. 13. "Traditionally, immigrants settled first in cities. But that's no longer true. Today they are more likely to go straight to midsize towns and underutilized suburban gaps. The 2000 census revealed that minorities were responsible for the majority of suburban population gains made in the 1990s" (David Brooks, *On Paradise Drive* [New York: Simon & Schuster, 2004], p. 35).

[23]See Rodney Clapp's *Families at the Crossroads* (Downers Grove, Ill.: InterVarsity Press, 1993).

[24]Andres Duany, Elizabeth Plater-Zyberk and Jeff Speck, *Suburban Nation* (New York: North Point Press, 2000), p. 44.

[25]Ibid., pp. 45-46.

[26]"Suburban Levittowners spent their weekends in individualizing their mass-produced homes," observes historian Gary Cross. They converted unfinished attics into additional bedrooms and remodeled basements into rec rooms and play areas for children. "Despite cookie-cutter construction for the homogenous mass market, wage-earning suburbanites often redesigned their houses to reflect their personality and lifestyles" (Gary Cross, "The Suburban Weekend," in *Visions of Suburbia,* ed. Roger Silverstone [New York: Routledge, 1997], pp. 112, 123).

[27]July 2004 prices (see Leon Lazaroff, "An Exodus from Suburbia?" *Chicago Tribune,* February 24, 2005, sec. 1, p. 9).

[28]Douglas Frantz and Catherine Collins, *Celebration, U.S.A.* (New York: Henry Holt, 1997), p. 5.

[29]Alex Marshall, *How Cities Work* (Austin: University of Texas Press, 2000), p. 14.

[30]Ibid., p. 39.

[31]Ibid., p. 26.

[32]Baxandall and Ewen, *Picture Windows*, p. 253. The town in the movie *The Truman Show* was reportedly modeled on Seaside.

[33]"Architect Sarah Susanka, author of the book *The Not So Big House*, says architecture 'can create all kinds of psychological responses.' Cathedrals and capitol buildings are designed to dwarf visitors—appropriate goals for these places, she says, but not for the living room" (Marianne Szegedy-Maszak, "Where Size Matters," *U.S. News & World Report*, June 28-July 5, 2004, p. 60).

[34]Data compiled by the United Nations and the U.S. Department of Energy (see Brooks, *Paradise Drive*, p. 80). American suburban single-family homes are "quite odd when viewed in a global context. There is not another nation on earth that houses its citizens as we do, and few could afford to" (Duany, Plater-Zyberk and Speck, *Suburban Nation*, p. 39).

[35]See Chiras and Wann, *Superbia!*

[36]Robert Banks, "Suburbia," in *The Complete Book of Everyday Christianity*, ed. Robert Banks and R. Paul Stevens (Downers Grove, Ill.: InterVarsity Press, 1997), pp. 984-85.

Chapter 3: Spaced Out

[1]J. John Palen, *The Suburbs* (New York: McGraw-Hill, 1995), p. xiii.

[2]Andres Duany, Elizabeth Plater-Zyberk and Jeff Speck, *Suburban Nation* (New York: North Point Press, 2000), p. 22.

[3]Such European cities often were walled compounds, necessitating maximum use of limited city space. With the exceptions of Quebec City and Montreal, cities in North America were built without physical walls, though Wall Street in Manhattan is named for a temporary barricade erected against Native Americans. (See Kenneth T. Jackson, *Crabgrass Frontier* [New York: Oxford University Press, 1985], pp. 14-15.)

[4]Palen, *Suburbs*, pp. 24, 27.

[5]Ford's cars were cheaper than European imports and were sturdier and easier to repair. By 1923 Kansas had more cars than France or Germany. "When Model T production finally ceased in 1927, the ownership of an automobile had reached the point of being an essential part of normal middle-class living" (Jackson, *Crabgrass Frontier*, pp. 161-62).

[6]Palen, *Suburbs*, p. 43.

[7]Prior to the car, most roads were made of dirt, intended for horses, filled with ruts and potholes. Cities were more than happy to embrace the automobile as a replacement for horses; "the private car was initially regarded as the very salva-

tion of the city, a clean and efficient alternative to the old-fashioned, manure-befouled, odoriferous, space-intensive horse" (Jackson, *Crabgrass Frontier,* pp. 163-64).

[8]"This was true even in the older suburbs having public transit. In fact, by the beginning of the 1930s, over half of the commuters in all but the largest cities already were driving to work. Commuters in New York and Chicago still relied primarily on mass transit lines, but most of those in Washington, Cincinnati, St. Louis, Milwaukee, Kansas City, and Los Angeles drove" (Palen, *Suburbs,* pp. 44-45).

[9]Tom Lewis, *Divided Highways* (New York: Penguin, 1997), p. x.

[10]Eric O. Jacobsen, *Sidewalks in the Kingdom* (Grand Rapids: Brazos, 2003), p. 24.

[11]John Handley, "Gas Costs Weigh on Drive to Work," *Chicago Tribune,* March 21, 2005, p. A1.

[12]Ibid.

[13]Duany, Plater-Zyberk and Speck, *Suburban Nation,* p. 23.

[14]Lewis, *Divided Highways,* p. x.

[15]Eric Jacobsen, "Eric O. Jacobsen on Urban Churches and Taking the Concrete Realities of Community Seriously," interview by Ken Myers, *Mars Hill Audio* 67 (March-April 2004).

[16]Albert Mehrabian, *Public Places and Private Spaces* (New York: Basic Books, 1976), pp. 316-17.

[17]Robert Banks, "Automobile," in *The Complete Book of Everyday Christianity,* ed. Robert Banks and R. Paul Stevens (Downers Grove, Ill.: InterVarsity Press, 1997), p. 54.

[18]"The obsessive concern with suburbs of houses on separate blocks arose from the early twentieth-century Western abhorrence of crowded city slums and the associated fear of disease and moral degeneracy" (Deborah Chambers, "A Stake in the Country: Women's Experiences of Suburban Development," in *Visions of Suburbia,* ed. Roger Silverstone [New York: Routledge, 1997], p. 87).

[19]From an interview with Robert Putnam <www.bowlingalone.com/media.php3>.

[20]Robert Putnam, *Bowling Alone* (New York: Simon & Schuster, 2000), p. 213.

[21]Barbara A. McCann and Reid Ewing, cited in "Sprawling Suburb, Hidden Belt Buckle," *Atlantic Monthly,* September 2004, p. 50.

[22]Cited in Amanda Spake, "Are the Burbs Killing You?" *U.S. News & World Report,* October 11, 2004, p. 35.

[23]Randy Frazee, *The Connecting Church* (Grand Rapids: Zondervan, 2001), p. 143. He argues, "In order to extract a deeper sense of belonging, we must consolidate our worlds into one. . . . The mission is to simplify our lifestyles in such a way that we concentrate more energy into a circle of relationships that produces a sense of genuine belonging" (ibid., pp. 34-35).

[24]M. Craig Barnes, *Searching for Home* (Grand Rapids: Brazos, 2003), p. 32; see Timothy Fry, ed., *The Rule of St. Benedict* (New York: Vintage, 1998), p. 56.

[25]John Ortberg, *The Life You've Always Wanted* (Grand Rapids: Zondervan, 1997), p. 81.

[26]Eric Jacobsen, "Eric O. Jacobsen on Urban Churches." Likewise, you might walk to a neighborhood grocery store and thus save gasoline on your personal commute, but if you buy fruits and vegetables that have been trucked in from across the country, you inadvertently contribute to the gasoline consumption for transporting the produce. This is one reason why many people prefer to shop at local farmers' markets. Not only is the produce fresher, it's also transported a shorter distance and thus consumes less resources.

[27]David Hansen, *Long Wandering Prayer* (Downers Grove, Ill.: InterVarsity Press, 2001), p. 54.

[28]Dr. Timothy Johnson, medical editor at ABC News, once told me about the findings of a national study of people who had once been obese but had lost over fifty pounds and kept it off for at least two years. While the subjects had used a variety of diets, it ultimately didn't seem to matter which kind of diet they followed. The common decisive factor was that they all exercised for at least an hour every day.

[29]From the U.S. Census Bureau report "Journey to Work: 2000," March 2004 <www.census.gov/prod/2004pubs/c2kbr-33.pdf>.

Chapter 4: Material World

[1]Roger Silverstone, ed., *Visions of Suburbia* (New York: Routledge, 1997), p. 8.

[2]As theologian Vincent Miller points out, "In contrast to previous forms of consumption that were enmeshed in a complicated division of labor among the extended family (e.g., small garden plots, maintaining livestock and poultry, and so on), standardized housing (now more spatially distant from the workplace) created a home sustained by the workings of technology and appliances (e.g., plumbing, cooking, light, heat, entertainment devices) that replace the labor of the extended family. These new technologies and appliances are also commodity-intensive because their functioning depends on an infrastructure of goods and services (e.g., coal, lamp oil, gasoline, electricity, plumbing, wiring, repair shops, and the like), that must be provided from the outside as well" (Vincent J. Miller, *Consuming Religion* [New York: Continuum, 2003], p. 46).

[3]Ibid., p. 50.

[4]Ibid., p. 48.

[5]Pope John Paul II, address at the 1999 World Day of Peace, cited in ibid., p. 15.

[6]Ibid., p. 16.

[7]Pope John Paul II, cited in ibid., p. 15.

[8]Ibid., pp. 185-86.

[9]"Ten Thousand Villages provides vital, fair income to Third World people by marketing their handicrafts and telling their stories in North America." Ten Thousand Villages is a nonprofit program of Mennonite Central Committee (MCC), the relief and development agency of Mennonite and Brethren in Christ churches in North America. For more information, see <www.tenthousandvillages.com>.

[10]Betsy Burton, "On Cost and Community," *Publishers Weekly,* August 22, 2005, p. 72.

[11]Rodney Clapp, *Border Crossings* (Grand Rapids: Brazos, 2000), p. 142.

[12]Ibid., p. 140.

[13]Juliet B. Schor, *The Overspent American* (New York: Basic Books, 1998), p. 161.

[14]Richard J. Foster, *Freedom of Simplicity* (San Francisco: Harper & Row, 1981), p. 121.

[15]Schor, *Overspent American,* p. 146.

[16]David Matzko McCarthy, *The Good Life* (Grand Rapids: Brazos, 2004), p. 97.

[17]Andy Crouch, "Live More Musically," *Christianity Today,* August 2004, p. 54.

[18]This thought is borrowed from Vincent Miller in an interview with Ken Meyers, "Vincent Miller, on How the Commodification of Everything Affects Our Sense of Religious Faith and Practice (and on How We Can Resist)," *Mars Hill Audio* 69 (July-August 2004).

[19]Michael Card, *Scribbling in the Sand* (Downers Grove, Ill.: InterVarsity Press, 2002), p. 37.

[20]Culture is "what we make of the world," both in the sense of creating artifacts and making sense of them. See Andy Crouch's forthcoming book, tentatively titled *Culture Makers,* to be released by InterVarsity Press in 2007 or 2008.

[21]Foster, *Freedom of Simplicity,* p. 118.

[22]Thomas N. Finger, *A Contemporary Anabaptist Theology* (Downers Grove, Ill.: InterVarsity Press, 2004), p. 249.

[23]Ibid., p. 238.

[24]C. S. Lewis, *God in the Dock* (Grand Rapids: Eerdmans, 1970), p. 216.

[25]Richard J. Foster, *Celebration of Discipline,* rev. ed. (San Francisco: HarperSanFrancisco, 1988), p. 87.

Chapter 5: Status Check

[1]James Howard Kunstler, *The Geography of Nowhere* (New York: Simon & Schuster, 1993).

[2]Press release, Harry Levine, "Dayton's and Southdale Stores," issued October 7, 1956, by Ruder & Finn, Incorporated <www.southdale.com/Stellent01/groups/public/@mallsouthdale/documents/webassets/029241.pdf>.

[3]Press release, Harry Levine, "Origins of Southdale," issued October 7, 1956, by

Ruder & Finn, Incorporated <www.southdale.com/stellent01/groups/public/@mall southdale/documents/webassets /029249.pdf>.

[4]Ibid.

[5]"History," Southdale Center <www.southdale.com/static/node2231.jsp>.

[6]Press release, "The Garden Court," issued October 7, 1956, by Ruder & Finn Incorporated <www.southdale.com/stellent01/groups/public/@mallsouthdale/docu ments/webassets/029246.pdf>.

[7]Ibid.

[8]Roger Silverstone, ed., *Visions of Suburbia* (New York: Routledge, 1997), p. 8.

[9]"Indeed, by default the mall has become downtown, the public space once occupied by Main Street, the Town Hall, or bustling retail city streets. Yet despite their convenience and glitzy appeal, malls have proven themselves a public space only in the most limited sense. . . . [M]alls play the role of town center only so far as profits are concerned" (Rosalyn Baxandall and Elizabeth Ewen, *Picture Windows* [New York: Basic Books, 2000], p. 228). See also Rodney Clapp, *Border Crossings* (Grand Rapids: Brazos, 2000), pp. 164-68.

[10]J. John Palen, *The Suburbs* (New York: McGraw-Hill, 1995), p. 99.

[11]James Twitchell, cited in Katy Kelly and Linda Kulman, "Kid Power," *U.S. News & World Report,* September 13, 2004, p. 48.

[12]Juliet Schor, cited in ibid., p. 47.

[13]As a result, "the United States, with 4.5 percent of the world's population, buys 45 percent of the global toy production" (ibid., p. 47).

[14]Ibid., p. 50.

[15]Ibid., p. 49.

[16]Juliet Schor, cited in ibid., pp. 48, 50.

[17]Malcolm Gladwell's influential book *The Tipping Point* (New York: Little, Brown, 2000) has a fascinating chapter on the "stickiness" of Blue's Clues and how the show creates amazing brand loyalty among preschoolers.

[18]Edward Hallowell, cited in Kelly and Kulman, "Kid Power," p. 48.

[19]James B. Twitchell, *Branded Nation* (New York: Simon & Schuster, 2004), p. 30.

[20]Ibid., p. 31.

[21]Ibid., p. 41.

[22]Sam Hill and Chris Lederer, *The Infinite Asset* (Boston: Harvard Business School Press, 2001), pp. 82-84, 89, 93.

[23]Twitchell, *Branded Nation,* p. 26.

[24]Neil Cummings and Marysia Lewandowska, cited in ibid., p. 37.

[25]Ibid., p. 36.

[26]Twitchell, cited in Kelly and Kulman, "Kid Power," p. 60.

[27]Stewart Brand notes that as people get older, they care less about fashion: "Adolescents

are obsessed with fashion, elders bored by it" (*The Clock of the Long Now* [New York: Basic Books, 2000], p. 36, cited in Andy Crouch's forthcoming book on culture).

[28]See Barbara Ehrenreich, *Nickel and Dimed* (New York: Metropolitan Books, 2001), chap. 3. According to a February 2004 report by the National Labor Committee, Chinese factory workers making plastic toys for Wal-Mart "worked for up to 20 hours a day, sometimes 7 days a week, for an average of 16.5 cents per hour; the legal minimum is 31 cents an hour" (Jeff M. Sellers, "Deliver Us from Wal-Mart?" *Christianity Today,* May 2005, p. 43).

[29]For more about Pura Vida Coffee, visit www.puravidacoffee.com or see chapter 9 in Steve Rundle and Tom Steffen, *Great Commission Companies* (Downers Grove, Ill.: InterVarsity Press, 2003).

[30]Tom Sine, "America's Culture Wars: In Search of a Third Way," *PRISM,* July-August 2004, available at the Mustard Seed Associates website at <www.msainfo.org /images/bank/156Americas_culture_wars.pdf>.

Chapter 6: Won't You Be My Neighbor?

[1]Ray Suarez, *The Old Neighborhood* (New York: Free Press, 1999), p. 4. These homes were bought on the G.I. Bill and had three bedrooms and two bathrooms. At the time, these new homes cost eighteen or twenty thousand dollars. Adjusted for inflation, that would be around $130,000 to $150,000 in today's dollars.

[2]Ibid., pp. 24-25.

[3]Between 1981 and 1997 the amount of time children spent in organized sports increased by 27 percent. "In 1981 U.S. Youth Soccer had 811,000 registered players. By 1998 it had nearly 3 million" (David Brooks, *On Paradise Drive* [New York: Simon & Schuster, 2004], p. 140).

[4]Suarez, *Old Neighborhood,* p. 19.

[5]Alex Marshall, *How Cities Work* (Austin: University of Texas Press, 2000), p. xvi. He continues, "Several factors working together have made it so people are both less obliged and less able to be physically tied to a specific neighborhood and city through a web of family, friendly, and economic relationships. The car and the highway have produced places that are fractured physically, and in the related patterns of commerce and business. The huge explosion of wealth in the last half-century has meant that more people can choose to leave a place if they choose. And a more global economy means people are less able to remain tied to a specific city or place" (ibid.).

[6]Faith Popcorn, *The Popcorn Report* (New York: Doubleday Currency, 1991), p. 28.

[7]Quentin J. Schultze, "Television," in *The Complete Book of Everyday Christianity,* ed. Robert Banks and R. Paul Stevens (Downers Grove, Ill.: InterVarsity Press, 1997), p. 1025.

[8]Ibid., p. 1026.

[9]Roger Silverstone, ed., *Visions of Suburbia* (New York: Routledge, 1997), p. 10.

[10]Ibid.

[11]Brooks, *Paradise Drive,* p. 50.

[12]J. John Palen, *The Suburbs* (New York: McGraw-Hill, 1995), pp. 97-98.

[13]Ibid., p. 85.

[14]Dolores Hayden, *Building Suburbia* (New York: Pantheon, 2003), p. 14. "We think of suburbs as places where families move to raise kids. But in fact, married couples with children make up only 27 percent of suburban households, according to the 2000 census. Today the suburbs contain more people living alone than families with kids" (Brooks, *Paradise Drive,* p. 5).

[15]"Today, the institute reports, the average child spends 31 hours a week with his or her mother, up from about 25 hours a week in 1980. The average child spends 23 hours a week with his or her father, up from 19 hours a week" (Brooks, *Paradise Drive,* p. 139).

[16]See Rodney Clapp's *Families at the Crossroads* (Downers Grove, Ill.: InterVarsity Press, 1993), on the church as first family and the biological family as second family.

[17]See Karen Miller and Kevin Miller, *More Than You and Me* (Colorado Springs: Focus on the Family, 1994), which argues that parents and children are all better off when they share service together outside their own families.

[18]Robert Putnam, in an interview posted on <www.bowlingalone.com/media.php3>.

[19]James B. Twitchell, *Branded Nation* (New York: Simon & Schuster, 2004), p. 275.

[20]Howard Schultz and Dori Jones Yang, *Pour Your Heart into It* (New York: Hyperion, 1997), p. 51.

[21]Ibid., p. 120.

[22]Ray Oldenburg, *The Great Good Place* (New York: Paragon, 1991), p. 16.

[23]Schultz and Yang, *Pour Your Heart into It,* p. 120.

[24]Ibid., pp. 120-21.

[25]Some authors have thanked their local Panera Bread or Caribou Coffee in the acknowledgments of their books and listed the employees by name. One such author's book was brought to the attention of a corporate executive, who held up the book at an employee convention and said, "This is customer service!"

[26]Bill Hybels and Mark Mittelberg, *Becoming a Contagious Christian* (Grand Rapids: Zondervan, 1994), p. 115.

[27]Alison J. Clarke, "Tupperware: Suburbia, Sociality and Mass Consumption," in *Visions of Suburbia,* ed. Roger Silverstone (New York: Routledge, 1997), p. 138.

[28]Ibid., p. 133.

[29]Ibid., p. 149.

[30]Ibid., pp. 144-45.

[31]While such parties are predominantly female, they are not exclusively so. I once hosted a Tupperware party in college, though I'm not sure it was really worth the presenter's time because I could only badger five or six people to come. More recently one of our friends, Kathy, was a Pampered Chef consultant and salesperson, and our pastor hosted a Pampered Chef party for the men of our church. Kathy told me afterward that the men bought more items and generated higher revenue per person than the average woman.

[32]Christine D. Pohl, *Making Room* (Grand Rapids: Eerdmans, 1999), pp. 8, 150.

[33]Richard J. Foster, *Freedom of Simplicity* (San Francisco: Harper & Row, 1981), p. 122.

Chapter 7: Finding God in the Suburbs

[1]Douglas Coupland, *Life After God* (New York: Pocket Books, 1994), pp. 271, 273.

[2]Craig M. Gay, *The Way of the (Modern) World* (Grand Rapids: Eerdmans, 1998), p. 13.

[3]Ibid., p. 2.

[4]Coupland, *Life After God,* p. 359.

[5]I read Coupland's novel more than a decade ago, and only now, while reflecting on the shift that takes place in the protagonist, did I realize that the title *Life After God* could have a double meaning. I have no idea if this was intentional on the part of the author, but the possibility opens up new layers of insight and meaning for me.

[6]David Brooks, *On Paradise Drive* (New York: Simon & Schuster, 2004), p. 6.

[7]Dallas Willard, *The Spirit of the Disciplines* (San Francisco: Harper & Row, 1988), p. 158.

[8]Roger Steer, *Guarding the Holy Fire* (Grand Rapids: Baker, 1999), p. 211.

[9]Michele Rickett and Kay Marshall Strom, *Daughters of Hope* (Downers Grove, Ill.: InterVarsity Press, 2003), pp. 190-91.

[10]Ibid., p. 187.

[11]Aleksandr I. Solzhenitsyn, *The Gulag Archipelago: 1918-1956,* trans. Thomas P. Whitney and Harry Willetts, abridg. Edward E. Ericson Jr. (New York: Perennial Classics, 2002), pp. 312-13.

[12]Richard J. Foster, *Freedom of Simplicity* (San Francisco: Harper & Row, 1981), p. 122.

[13]Ibid.

[14]An actual name-it-and-claim-it prayer, recorded in Patton Dodd, *My Faith So Far* (San Francisco: Jossey-Bass, 2005), p. 121.

[15]Barbara Brown Taylor, *When God Is Silent* (Cambridge, Mass.: Cowley, 1998), pp. 9-10.

[16]Bill McKibben, *The Comforting Whirlwind* (Grand Rapids: Eerdmans, 1994), p. 37.

[17]Ibid., p. 82.

[18]See Eric Schlosser, *Fast Food Nation* (New York: Houghton Mifflin, 2001), p. 47.

[19]"Perhaps someday, like my church, I will learn to share my home with little creatures, as I am learning to share it with little people" (Bethany Torode, "From *Ewww* . . . to *Wow!*" *Christianity Today,* December 2004, p. 58, see also <www.christianity today.com/ct/2004/012/18.58.html>.

[20]Eugene Peterson, in the foreword to Eric Jacobsen, *Sidewalks in the Kingdom* (Grand Rapids: Brazos, 2003), p. 10.

[21]Ruth Haley Barton, *Invitation to Solitude and Silence* (Downers Grove, Ill.: InterVarsity Press, 2004), pp. 34-35.

[22]Henri Nouwen, *The Way of the Heart* (San Francisco: HarperSanFrancisco, 1981), pp. 34-39.

[23]Brother Lawrence, cited in *Devotional Classics,* ed. Richard J. Foster and James Bryan Smith (San Francisco: HarperSanFrancisco, 1993), p. 82.

[24]See my devotion on this theme, "The God Who Recycles," in Robert Boyd Munger's *My Heart—Christ's Home Through the Year,* ed. David A. Zimmerman and Cindy Bunch (Downers Grove, Ill.: InterVarsity Press, 2004), p. 201.

[25]One of the key factors motivating me to keep a daily journal was Bob Greene's book *Be True to Your School* (New York: Atheneum, 1987), which I read just before my junior year of high school, based on his diary from his junior and senior year of high school. He writes in the preface, "When I looked at the diary after years had passed, I realized that what I had here was something money could not buy: time preserved" (ibid., p. vii). His entries recorded all the volatility of the high school years, the emotions that radically changed from day to day. I was experiencing that myself at the time I read Greene's book, and a similar experience is true for me when I look back at my old journals.

[26]A good resource for the practice and spiritual discipline of journaling is Luann Budd's *Journal Keeping* (Downers Grove, Ill.: InterVarsity Press, 2002).

[27]Phyllis Tickle's *The Divine Hours,* 3 vols. (New York: Doubleday, 2000-2001) and Robert Benson's *Venite: A Book of Daily Prayer* (New York: Tarcher/Putnam, 2000) are excellent resources for fixed-hour prayer.

[28]This is an area in which Christians can learn much from Muslims. The Islamic pillar of daily prayer at five particular points of time is a practice that orders, shapes and orients daily life for Muslims. It's significant that Muslim converts to Christianity often continue this practice by adopting Christian practices of fixed-hour prayer.

Chapter 8: The Suburban Church

[1]Leith Anderson, *A Church for the 21st Century* (Minneapolis: Bethany House, 1992), p. 119.

[2]Lynne Hybels and Bill Hybels, *Rediscovering Church* (Grand Rapids: Zondervan, 1995), p. 57.

[3]James B. Twitchell, *Branded Nation* (New York: Simon & Schuster, 2004), p. 91.

[4]Ibid., p. 84.

[5]Ibid., p. 85.

[6]Ibid., p. 278.

[7]Robert D. Putnam and Lewis M. Feldstein with Don Cohen, *Better Together* (New York: Simon & Schuster, 2003), p. 124.

[8]Twitchell, *Branded Nation,* p. 279.

[9]Ibid., p. 84.

[10]Ken Dean, "Building the Emerging Church," *The Church Report,* June 2005 <www.thechurchreport.com/content/view/423/32>.

[11]Ken Dean, "The Third Place Power for Connection," *The Church Report*, April 2005 <www.thechurchreport.com/content/view/323/0>.

[12]Twitchell, *Branded Nation,* p. 75.

[13]Joseph Turow, *Breaking Up America* (Chicago: University of Chicago Press, 1997), p. 106. He writes, "In the highly competitive media environment of the 1980s and early 1990s, cable companies aiming to lure desirable types to specialized formats have felt the need to create 'signature' materials that both drew the 'right' people and signaled the 'wrong' people that they ought to go away. It is no accident that the producers of certain signature programs on Nickelodeon (for example, *The Ren and Stimpy Show*) and MTV (such as *Beavis and Butt-Head*) in the early 1990s acknowledge that they chase away irrelevant viewers as much as they attract desirable ones" (ibid., p. 5).

[14]Ray Bakke, *The Urban Christian* (Downers Grove, Ill.: InterVarsity Press, 1987), p. 128.

[15]Eugene Peterson, "Spirituality for All the Wrong Reasons," interview by Mark Galli, *Christianity Today,* March 2005, p. 47.

[16]Ibid.

[17]Ibid., p. 45.

[18]See Dan Kimball, *The Emerging Church* (Grand Rapids: Zondervan, 2003), esp. p. 185; as well as Robert Webber's *The Younger Evangelicals* (Grand Rapids: Baker, 2002); and Colleen Carroll's *The New Faithful* (Chicago: Loyola Press, 2002).

[19]I heard of a family with four kids who were horrendously overscheduled with multiple activities. The parents wisely told their kids that they could each do only one

extracurricular activity a semester. Even so, that still meant that there were four things to keep up with each week, and the parents still ended up spending much of their time ferrying kids back and forth to activities.

[20]For more information about the contemplative approach to youth ministry, see The Youth Ministry and Spirituality Project <www.ymsp.org>. See also Mike King's *Presence-Centered Youth Ministry* (Downers Grove, Ill.: InterVarsity Press, 2006).

[21]Etan Diamond, *And I Will Dwell in Their Midst* (Chapel Hill: The University of North Carolina Press, 2000), p. 9.

[22]Ibid., pp. 22, 18.

[23]One man lamented to me that his church's neighborhood was changing and that many of his church members were deciding to move to "safer" suburbs farther away. He wondered aloud if there was any way to rebuke his fellow church members for what was likely racial prejudice against the new neighbors. My response was, "You know, it might be better to cast a positive vision for living in the community that they worship in. Make them see that living far away from their church is harmful to them, the church and the community." That way they might come to see the changing demographics as a gift and opportunity to learn to love their new neighbors.

[24]Greg Ligon, "Inside the Multi-Site Revolution," *Leadership Network Advance,* May 24, 2005 <www.pursuantgroup.com/leadnet/advance/may05s2a.htm>. Ligon quotes Larry Osborne of North Coast Church in Vista, California: "Along with eliminating the need for ever bigger buildings, [multisite] allows a regional church to take the church to the people rather than asking them to drive in from farther and farther distances. They have all the advantages of a neighborhood church with the backing and programs of a regional church" (ibid.).

[25]See Community Christian Church's website at <www.communitychristian.org>.

[26]This is a truth that Christians throughout the ages have held, from Augustine to Calvin to Merton. See David Benner, *The Gift of Being Yourself* (Downers Grove, Ill.: InterVarsity Press, 2004), chap. 1.

Chapter 9: Beyond Suburbia

[1]Gaylord B. Noyce, *The Responsible Suburban Church* (Philadelphia: Westminster Press, 1970), p. 14.

[2]Stephen Goldsmith, *The Twenty-First Century City* (Washington, D.C.: Regnery, 1997), p. 85.

[3]Ibid.

[4]Eric Swanson, "Social Capital and the Externally Focused Church" <www.pursuant group.com/leadnet/into_action/0404_b.htm>. See Robert D. Putnam, *Bowling*

Alone (New York: Simon & Schuster, 2000), pp. 22-24.

[5]Robert Wuthnow, cited in ibid., p. 78.

[6]Swanson, "Social Capital."

[7]John R. Schneider, "Can Christianity Engage Consumer Capitalism?" *Pro Rege* 33, no. 3 (2005): 12.

[8]Corinth may have had a population of about eighty thousand and another twenty thousand in its "suburbs" of smaller cities, towns and villages in the surrounding area (Eckhard J. Schnabel, *Early Christian Mission* [Downers Grove, Ill.: InterVarsity Press, 2004], p. 1183). Thessalonica was the capital and most populous city in Macedonia. Scholars estimate the population as being between twenty to forty thousand inhabitants in the first century, or perhaps sixty-five thousand in the city and a total of one hundred thousand if surrounding villages are included (ibid., pp. 1160, 1162).

[9]Richard Lamb, *Following Jesus in the "Real World"* (Downers Grove, Ill.: InterVarsity Press, 1995), pp. 26-27.

[10]Singles may have a missional gift of mobility, while families may have the complementary missional gift of hospitality. Going and sending work together. See my thoughts on this in Albert Y. Hsu, *Singles at the Crossroads* (Downers Grove, Ill.: InterVarsity Press, 1997), especially chap. 5 and pp. 134-36.

[11]Henri J. M. Nouwen, Donald P. McNeil and Douglas A. Morrison, *Compassion* (New York: Doubleday, 1982), p. 64.

[12]Ibid., p. 71.

[13]Ibid., p. 70.

[14]Ibid., pp. 73-74.

[15]Robert D. Lupton, *Renewing the City* (Downers Grove, Ill.: InterVarsity Press, 2005), pp. 224-25.

[16]See Robert Linthicum, *Transforming Power* (Downers Grove, Ill.: InterVarsity Press, 2003), for more about the dynamics of community organizing and the responsible exercise of relational power.

[17]Lupton, *Renewing the City,* p. 226.

[18]Walter Brueggemann, *Peace* (St. Louis: Chalice, 2001), pp. 28-29.

[19]See Cornelius Plantinga Jr., *Not the Way It's Supposed to Be* (Grand Rapids: Eerdmans, 1995), p. 10.

[20]David Brooks, *On Paradise Drive* (New York: Simon & Schuster, 2004), p. 80.

[21]Jeremy Weber, "Raising the Compassion Bar," *Christianity Today,* August 2005, pp. 50-52. For more information on AIDS Student Network, see <www.aidsstudent network.org>.

[22]Peggy Wehmeyer, "Selling the Family on an Unspoiled Christmas," *Morning Edition,* National Public Radio, December 20, 2004 <www.npr.org/templates/story

/story.php?storyId=4235929>. An example of these gift catalogs is World Vision's <www.giftsofhope.org>.

Epilogue

[1]The Blessing from Morning Prayer, in The Northumbria Community, *Celtic Daily Prayer* (San Francisco: HarperSanFrancisco, 2002), p. 19.

Index

abundance, affluence, 12, 48, 82-83, 93, 102, 139-40, 143, 184, 189-92, 193

advertising, 37, 40, 82-83, 85, 101, 102-3, 105-7, 108-9, 111, 166

air conditioning, 119

automobiles/cars, 22, 33, 43, 48, 51, 57-60, 61-63, 71-73, 75, 92, 121, 148, 206n. 5

Blue's Clues, 103-4, 111, 210n. 17

branding, 24, 58, 84, 96-97, 101-9, 124-25, 160, 162, 165-66, 168

Brueggemann, Walter, 189-91

carpooling, 51, 72-73

Celebration, Florida, 47-49, 50

Chesterton, G. K., 92

churches, 19, 52, 58, 67, 72, 90, 114, 129, 142, 149, 156-76, 177, 179-81, 186-88, 192-95
  architecture of, 157-59
  brand identities of, 105, 109, 165-69, 171
  contextualization of, 159-62, 169-72, 175, 202n. 4

cities
  biblical, 181, 217n. 8
  history of, 25, 27, 56, 204n. 24
  of refuge, 189
  suburbanization of, 15-16, 21-22

theology of, 28-29

civic involvement, 30-31, 52-53, 81, 128, 162-63, 179-80, 184

cocooning, 118, 124

cohousing, 51-52

Columbia, Maryland, 50

commodification, 74-75, 77-79, 84, 104, 105, 113

Community Christian Church, 164-65, 174

community, 11, 35, 47-49, 51-52, 62-63, 112, 117-18, 122, 124-25, 126-28, 132-36, 151, 162-64, 172-74, 186-88, 211n. 5

commuting, commuter culture, 24, 48, 50, 54-73
  alternatives to, 67-73
  history of, 56-58
  impact on health, 63-64
  time spent commuting, 55, 60, 63

Congress for a New Urbanism, 49

consumerism, consumption, 71, 74-94, 101-5, 110-13, 113-15, 139-40
  alternatives to, 83-84, 85-94
  and church, 160-62
  as ideology, 76-78

creativity, 75-77, 87-89, 131-32, 146

Disney theme parks, 105, 107, 125

Disney, Walt, 47-48

displacement, 30, 142, 184-86

ducks, 66, 147, 149

eBay, 104, 125

efficiency, 70, 109, 201

EPCOT, theme park, 47

Epcot, utopian city, 47, 48

exurbs, 21, 23, 36, 60, 122

fair trade coffee, 79, 113-14

farmers' markets, 79, 208n. 26

fast food, 76, 79, 112, 146

fasting, 73, 86, 148

Federal Housing Administration, 34

front porches, 43, 47-48, 119, 122

garages, 35, 51-52, 92, 119, 135

gated communities, 45

generosity, 89-91, 93, 144

global issues and mission, 26, 30, 31, 46, 77-80, 86, 114, 139-42, 181, 184-85, 193-96, 199, 206n. 35, 209n. 9

Great Depression, 33, 35, 57

green space, 52, 62, 146

Habitat for Humanity, 52

hospitality, 52, 124, 128, 132-36, 186, 217n. 10

housing, 23, 32, 33-36, 38-40, 43, 45-47, 50, 52, 75, 92-93

identity, 39, 42, 67, 78, 97, 102, 106-7, 110-13, 124-25, 167-68, 176

independent businesses, 79, 81-82, 96

individualism, 39-40, 43, 51, 58, 75, 106, 187-88

intentional living communities, 52, 112, 182

interstate highways, Interstate Highway Act, 33, 34, 57, 60-61, 203n. 12

isolationism, 40, 43, 45-46, 75, 117-19, 122, 128

journaling, 154, 214n. 25

justice, 31, 42, 52, 77-80, 111, 113-15, 167, 177-78, 187-89, 196

Lawrence, Brother, 153

lemonade stands, 135

Levittown, 34, 36, 46-47,